Responding to the Light

Reflections on
Advent, Christmas and Epiphany

In memory of Clifford and Sally Betts

Responding to the Light

Reflections on
Advent, Christmas and Epiphany

Michael Mayne

Edited, with an Introduction,
by
Joel W. Huffstetler

CANTERBURY
PRESS
Norwich

© The estate of Michael Mayne, 2017
Introduction © Joel Huffstetler, 2017

First published in 2017 by the Canterbury Press Norwich
Editorial office
3rd Floor, Invicta House
108–114 Golden Lane
London EC1Y 0TG, UK

Second impression 2018

Canterbury Press is an imprint of Hymns Ancient & Modern Ltd
(a registered charity)

Hymns Ancient & Modern® is a registered trademark of
Hymns Ancient & Modern Ltd
13A Hellesdon Park Road, Norwich
Norfolk NR6 5DR, UK

www.canterburypress.co.uk

British Library Cataloguing in Publication data

A catalogue record for this book is available
from the British Library

978 1 84825 980 5

Typeset by Manila Typesetting Company
Printed and bound in Great Britain by
CPI Group (UK) Ltd

Contents

Part I – Advent

Part II – Christmas

Part III – Epiphany

Foreword

The poet R.S. Thomas believed that poetry is that 'which arrives at the intellect by way of the heart'. The same can be said of a sermon. The preacher begins by declaring war on cliché and then conscripts words and images that resist the quick clarity of relevance in order to find resonance, words from which we cannot retreat. Those who dare to preach are brave. They are called to dispel human illusions without leaving them disillusioned. They invite the world to be re-imagined. They are willing to sound sadly implausible as they push the words 'God', 'mystery', 'love' and 'eternity' back into a landscape that has very nearly lost the echoes. And because theology is what happens on the way to the pulpit, the preacher discovers what he or she believes most deeply in this rich, complex process of sermon–shaping. It is an intensely personal enterprise in an alarmingly public arena.

Michael Mayne was an exemplary preacher. He was a friend and I heard him preach many times. Unafraid to acknowledge darkness, his faith compelled him to believe that reality is ultimately trustworthy, an endless sequence of variations on the unchanging themes of God's love and energy. He preached from his scars and not his wounds. In the pulpit, he was discernibly modest but confident in his calling. He was unafraid to reason but unashamed to adore. He was there primarily to form not inform, to nurture a people able to think critically, live faithfully and love purposefully. Hearing Michael preach was to be encouraged as an apprentice of Christ by a wise soul aware of his own fault lines and fragility.

Sermons are events, not scripts: on the page something of their light dims. Reading a play is never the same as being there on the first night. In this collection, though, you encounter something of Michael and his holy reticence as well as the hope of his Christian vision. The seasons of Advent, Christmas and Epiphany bring this out, perhaps, even more than usual: Advent reminding us that for the Christian all things are as yet unfinished and the life of faith is one of longing, a life in the vocative. Christmas celebrates the God who comes to touch us into life because we are unable to heal ourselves and so to be saved from ourselves love must come from outside into our darkest places of possible birth. Epiphany acclaims these truths for everyone and not just for the pure, initiated or religious. These were the seasons in Michael's heart and which shaped his refreshing faith. This book is a beautiful witness to the fact.

Michael believed that love is holy because, like grace, the worthiness of its object is never really what matters. He knew that the Gospel, at the end of the day, is a message of fidelity towards us. He loved literature, theatre and the arts because, although we can't always understand them, they understand us and take us nearer to our private realities. He loved the scriptures and how they are opened up by human experience. He loved God, hidden, elusive, but communicating in presence and love.

In 1619 Bishop Lancelot Andrewes said in a sermon that our charge is to preach to people *'non quae volunt audire, sed quae volunt audisse'*, not what for the present they would hear but what in another day they would wish they had heard. Michael Mayne fulfilled the task.

Mark Oakley
July 2017

Acknowledgements

This new collection of sermons by Michael Mayne would not exist were it not for the assistance and support offered by Alison Mayne. Thank you Alison for your encouragement of and help with this project.

The staff of Sarum College, Salisbury, were gracious hosts during my stay there for portions of April and May 2016. Thanks in particular to Jenny Monds, Linda Cooper, James Woodward, David Catchpole, Patrick Moore, Seb Snook and Ralph Lever.

Martyn and Emma Percy were gracious in inviting me to stay and work in their home in Oxford for a week in April 2016. Martyn and Emma, thank you for your every kindness. Thanks also to Dan and Sarah Mayne Tyndall for a delightful and memorable weekend in Bristol.

Much of the final editing of this collection took place in June 2016 at the beach house of Andrea and Hal Roe. Thank you, dear friends, for your generous hospitality, and especially for the instructions on how to work the remote control!

Thanks to Christine Smith, Publishing Director of Hymns Ancient & Modern, for your enthusiastic embrace of and support for this project. Working with you and your team is a pleasure.

Thank you to the people of St Luke's Episcopal Church, Cleveland, Tennessee for your generous gift of sabbatical time 5 April to 5 July 2016. Debbie and I will never forget your kindness and support.

My wife Debbie has been my partner in this project from start to finish. Thank you, my love.

All editor's royalties are donated to Horatio's Garden, Salisbury Hospital in honour of Alison Mayne and in memory of Michael Mayne.

Joel W. Huffstetler
Cleveland, Tennessee
Easter Sunday, 2017

Introduction

The addresses collected in this volume were given by Michael Mayne (b.1929, d.2006) from 1987–2003. Most were offered in Westminster Abbey, though others were given in cathedrals and parish churches throughout England. All except for the final address, 'Commonplace *and* Awesome', were offered during Mayne's tenure as dean of Westminster Abbey, 1986–1996.

In reading these addresses one recognizes that they are timeless, as fresh and relevant as when first offered. Many of his hearers remember Michael Mayne as the finest preacher they have ever known. The addresses in this volume are a testament to his extraordinary giftedness with the spoken word.

Preachers of any time, place, or tradition will draw inspiration from these addresses which are so thoughtfully and carefully crafted. That said, Michael Mayne was always intentional that his words speak to all listeners, clergy or laity, those of deep faith or none. Michael Mayne was a consummate communicator, a consummate pastoral voice. Through these newly collected addresses he continues to speak.

This volume is the first in a trilogy of newly collected and published seasonal addresses by Michael Mayne. *Dust that Dreams of Glory* (Lent) and *Forward in Hope* (Easter and Pentecost) are forthcoming.

PART I

Advent

1

Respond to the Light

Now is the time to wake out of sleep! Romans 13.11

Prepared for what? For Christmas? Yes, certainly: prepared in all the busy-ness to give proper attention to this birth which reveals God as Christlike. And equally to reflect on the meaning of that unimaginable day when the book of history is closed and Christ is revealed as judge of the living and the dead. To look back to Christmas: to look forward to the final judgement. And to understand afresh that it is the Christlike God who is both our Saviour and our Judge.

Now that is fine – providing we remember those more immediate truths that the Church has always known: that we don't worship an absentee Christ who has come and gone again and may one day return, but the Christ who is present in his Spirit wherever his followers meet – the Christ encountered in people, in acts of love, in prayer, in the breaking of bread. And as for JUDGEMENT we are judged *now daily* – indeed we pass judgements on ourselves – by our actions and words and relationships, all of which show whether we choose to stay shut up in our own lonely darkness or respond to the light. Indeed, the gospel reminds us that our daily response to the poor, the homeless, the starving and the imprisoned is mysteriously but undeniably our response to Christ who is to be found (for those with eyes to see) in what Mother Teresa calls 'the distressing disguise' of the poorest and most marginalized members of society. So Advent, with its reminder of these truths, can be an uncomfortable season.

But perhaps the real importance of Advent is in its reminder that as there was a beginning of creation, so there will be an end; and as there is a beginning to our lives, so we each will die. But what do we mean by 'the end'? For the Bible 'the end' doesn't mean a final full stop, like the running of the credit titles before the empty screen at the end of the evening's viewing. It means the *purpose*, the end for which you and I and the whole universe were made, our proper and satisfying completion. The end for you and me is not extinction. Our purpose, our destiny, our proper end, is to come to know God himself, to respond with trust to his love in Jesus Christ, to respond with proper care, compassion and understanding to one another, and so find at last our completion, our fulfilment and our wholeness, as those who are made in God's likeness.

But if part of our ultimate fulfilment is to lose our lonely isolation in the company of heaven, so the purpose of the world, the *end* of history, is the establishment of the Kingdom of God. That is what Jesus came to proclaim: God's Kingdom. He lived it, preached it, suffered for it, died for it. And his victory over death was the greatest witness to its reality. His life and death and resurrection demonstrate once and for all the victory of good over evil. The Kingdom he reveals – life as God would have it – is the guarantee that war and disease and poverty are a violation of God's will, and that in the end – however long it takes – good will triumph over evil, truth over the lie, freedom and justice over oppression, love over hate, light over darkness. That is our vision, our hope, the end we pray for every time we say 'thy Kingdom come, thy will be done, on earth as it is in heaven.'

Advent hope is much more than a political and social hope for freedom and prosperity. It is the hope of the Kingdom of God – the Kingdom which is to be fulfilled in God's good time and in ways we cannot yet imagine. But a Kingdom too which since the first Christmas is already among us, a Kingdom of which every Eucharist is a tiny foretaste, and the Kingdom which (once our eyes are opened) keeps on breaking in in the most surprising ways and the most unexpected places.

2

The Window into God

Your sins are forgiven . . . go in peace. Luke 7.48–50

I don't know how long children's Advent calendars have been around. They take the form of a stable with 24 little closed windows, and you're supposed to open one window each day leading up to Christmas. The excitement for a young child is that anything may lie behind those windows: a dinosaur, perhaps, or a dragon, or a penguin. Of course you soon learn that it's all pretty predictable: there aren't that many possible permutations on a theme of stars and snowflakes, shepherds, cows and donkeys. But the final window is always the baby lying in a manger, the one who for Christians became the true, authentic window into that ultimate mystery we call God.

For 1,500 years the Western Church has kept Advent, not simply as a season of preparation for Christmas, but as a time to consider the mystery of death and judgement. For when all the other windows in our lives have been thrown open one by one to reveal the people and places that form our particular story, these windows of death and judgement remain closed, firmly bolted and barred from the outside, and we can only speculate about what may lie behind them like children who lie in bed and speculate about what may be lurking out there in the dark.

Or so it has seemed to many men and women down the ages. Yet Christians tell a rather different story. We don't deny the mystery. No human mind can conceive the nature of heaven or begin to imagine what a final judgement day could be like. And yet, because of what is revealed behind that final window of the Advent calendar, we see even the darkness in a different light: in the light of Christmas, of what we call the incarnation, in the light of this child's birth and life and teaching and suffering and death and rising.

Now let me word this very carefully and without prevarication, for this is a life-changing truth. Christianity is not about the trivia of our lives: it's about their ultimate purpose. Either what it claims touches our very centre and profoundly changes the way we see everything – or it is a comforting but ultimately irrelevant story that changes nothing. For if God was *not* in Christ and our faith is a delusion – if there is nothing behind that final window – then we are born into a chancy and precarious universe with no ultimate purpose or destiny; but if Christ *was* in very truth the window into God, then we are held in being in our lives and through our deaths by that loving creative Spirit whom he taught us to call Father, and who has created us to know and love him even as we are loved and known.

Now that is not the kind of truth you can grasp and live by all at once. Most of us need a lifetime to be so fully persuaded of it that it becomes as natural to us as breathing. But it is a truth that changes entirely our understanding of death and judgement.

For what does the day of judgement mean? I can know nothing of some remote and terrible *day* of judgement. I know simply that my judge is also my saviour. I know simply that day by day, ever since that final window was opened into God, I am judged, and I am judged chiefly on that commandment that is summed up in Christ's words: 'Love your neighbour as you love yourself.' And as St Paul writes: 'Remember how critical the moment is.' It is not in some unimaginable future, it is in the *now*, in the day called *today*, by my words and thoughts and actions, that I am opening or closing myself to the Spirit of love that was once and for all defined in the person of Jesus Christ. The New Testament never in fact speaks of *second* coming. It speaks of the coming of Christ, begun at Christmas, perfected on the cross, and continuing until all are included in it. It says that Christ is present through his Spirit in us, but is also to be found in the most unexpected people and places: not least in the homeless, the sick, the imprisoned. And it says that in the end Christ will come into everything and be seen to be what Christians claim he is already: our Lord and our judge.

The metaphor for God's judgement I like best was used by the prophet Amos who saw God standing before a wall with a plumbline in his hand, that cord used by a builder with a lead weight at one end that always hangs straight and true. The plumbline doesn't turn and condemn the wall, it just hangs true to its nature and simply by being itself shows up that which is warped or distorted.

So I do not believe there is a final window, only to be opened at some unknown time, which will reveal to our amazed eyes some form of judgement we don't already know. Simply by being himself Jesus discloses the true nature of self-giving love, of compassion, of forgiveness and mercy, truth and justice, once and for all. He doesn't give us a host of rules. Nor does he turn and condemn us. He simply – but at what a cost – shows us what it means to commit yourself to the way of love, and then meets our *repeated* failure to do so and our repentance with the judgement of those healing words: 'Your sins are forgiven: go in peace.'

3

A Wondering Silence

After me comes one mightier than I am, whose sandals I am not worthy to stoop down and unfasten. Mark 1.7

Marvellous, humble words of a disturbing figure, John the Baptist, who stands in the desert and quotes what Isaiah said about one who would come as a voice crying in the wilderness of his times. 'I am that voice', says John, but he draws attention not to himself but to Christ, the one who is about to reveal God in a new and definitive way.

I remember giving my grandson an Advent calendar, with its two dozen closed windows, one to be opened each day between the first Sunday of Advent and Christmas. As a child he thought that all sorts of exciting things might lie behind those windows, a dragon, perhaps, or a penguin or a dinosaur. He soon discovered the more predictable reality of stars and shepherds and donkeys, and that the final window opens on the baby lying in the manger, the one who for us became the true, authentic window into the mystery we call God. Yet what could be less predictable and more full of wonder than that God should so reveal himself in human terms, in the only language we can understand?

Christian leaders are to point to that amazing, life-changing truth that lies at the far end of Advent, for once you let that truth into your mind and heart it has to change the way you see everything else. If God was not in Christ, if there is nothing in that final window of the Advent calendar but a charming fairy tale, then we are all wasting our time. But if God *was* in Christ, and we accept that Jesus, alone of all our race, looked full at the transcendent mystery and said his name was Father, then we are able to trust that in our lives, and through our deaths, we are held in being by that loving creative Spirit who has made us in order that we may come to know and love him, even as we are loved and known for the unique individuals we are. What gives each one of us our true value in the eyes of God is that each of us is uniquely different and therefore literally irreplaceable.

A painter doesn't persuade or hector or try to manipulate you. A painter simply shows you what things look like in his or her eyes. An artist says: 'Pay attention! Come and see how even the most unlikely subject matter is transformed when the light falls on it in a certain way.' A Christian says: 'Come and see what God looks like, and what people look like, in the light of Christ.'

If I look at that arresting figure of John the Baptist and hear his words about 'the one whose sandal straps he is not worthy to unloose', and then turn my gaze to the scene 30 years later in an upper room, I find the most amazing thing of all. For I see the Christ kneel on the dusty floor, undo the straps of his friends' shoes and begin to wash their feet. And in so doing he changes for ever our whole understanding of the nature of God and the meaning of the life of faith.

Here is a God who reveals his nature by kneeling at our feet. For that is what love always does when faced with human need. And it is that proper love, that love of the merciful and Christlike God, that should reduce us all to a wondering silence, and by which one day we shall ourselves be judged.

4

I Give You My Word

Come to me and listen to my words; hear me and you shall live.
Isaiah 55.3

The Bible, the gospel, is about God communicating with us through his *word*, and I can think of no better phrase to sum up the heart of our faith than: 'I give you my word.' For consider: When I say 'I give you my word' I am saying two things. First and foremost I am saying: I want to take some bit of truth that is important to me and share it with you by framing it in the most meaningful words I can find. I want to take an invisible thought, a feeling, a belief, and flesh it out in words that may strike a chord in your own minds and hearts. But the words have got to be true words: they have to come from my own centre, from my heart, if they are not to be banalities that cost me nothing. That is to say, unless I give you something of myself, unless it is a costly activity, a tiny act of love, and unless you respond by giving me something of yourself, then there's no real communication, and nothing has been shared.

Now if that is true of us, then it must also be true of the God in whose image we are made. He wants to communicate to us his creatures something of his own inner nature, to give us his word, so that we have some idea of what he is like. So the Old Testament describes a God who speaks. He emerged, say the Jewish rabbinic texts, out of a profound silence and said, 'Let there be light.' And, according to Genesis, his word took the form of an emerging creation as chaos gives way to order, and his word is discerned in the slow unfolding panorama of a universe of such beauty and power as to ravish the senses. We find that aspect of God reflected in the psalms or the book of Job.

'I give you my word', says God, and civilizations rise and fall, until eventually there emerges a particular nation, Israel, and within that nation particular men – Abraham, Moses, Joshua – who, while protesting their own inability to speak for God, are nevertheless responsive to his word, and proclaim it. 'I give you my word', says God through prophets like Isaiah who speak for him and say: 'Come to me and listen to my words; hear me and you shall live.'

But the words of life fall on deaf ears and so, in a different and spectacular way, God says: 'I give you my word. I give you myself.' For as we hear in St John's great opening to his Gospel: 'In the beginning was the Word', in Greek, the Logos, the perfect expression of himself: 'and the Word was made flesh.' Through his Word, says St John, God creates all that exists. Through his Word he reveals himself to us in the only language we can understand. In a sovereign act of love the Word, God's expression of his inner nature in utterly human and unmistakable terms, is sent among us. God is saying, 'In Jesus, I give you my Word' – and the words of Jesus are backed by his life. So he can say to the Pharisees: 'The word has found no home in you, for you do not believe the one whom he sent.'

So God's self-portrait, God's Word, turns out at once to be more ordinary and more extraordinary than anyone had dreamed. As ordinary as the man in the village carpenter's shop: as extraordinary as every human being made in the divine image is shown by this man to be, when we turn and open ourselves in trust and gratitude to our Father's love.

I said at the start that when I say, 'I give you my word', I am saying two things. The first is that I give you a truth that lies deep at my centre and which I want to share with you, as God does in Christ, his Word made flesh. But there is a second meaning to that phrase, for 'I give you my word' can also mean, 'You can trust me.' 'Word of honour, I am speaking the truth, cross my heart and hope to die.' 'I give you my word.'

Which is, of course, what God is also saying in Jesus. For in Christ we may hear God saying:

Trust me. I give you my word that you are loved. Even when that doesn't seem to be possible: even when life is at its darkest. I am the God who is beside you and whose life is within you, beside you in your joys and in your afflictions, at all times and in all places, and beside you eventually in your dying and through and beyond your death. For I too, in my Word that was once made flesh, know what it is to live, to suffer and to die. Trust me. I give you my word.

5

The Divine Mercy

For your part, stand by the truths you have learned and are assured of.
2 Timothy 3.14

One of the perils of my time as dean of Westminster was having to go to large dinners where you knew nothing of your immediate neighbours. 'Tell me about yourself', I would say at the start of what might prove to be a very long meal. And I would then learn where they were born and grew up and what they did for a living, and what their children did, and where they went on holiday and even (on bad nights) the make of their car and the name of their dog.

But all that had to do with what I call our public journey, that part of our lives that is concerned with what we *do*, with places and events and jobs, with achievements and possessions: and all that is hugely important. Until the moment when we come to die. For then the only journey that will have mattered is that other, different journey: the inner, private journey. That journey that has to do with quite other and much more difficult words, words like trust and hope and wonder, words like pain and loneliness and grief, words like forgiveness, and steadfast love. And if you are a Christian, then such words take on a new dimension, and you know your life is also a journey into mystery, a pilgrimage of faith, an exploration of the nature of the Christlike God and your relationship with him. And, in the end, though of course they interrelate, it is this inner, private journey which is the only journey that counts. Not what I possess, or even what I have done, but what I *am*, what I have become.

I call it 'private', but it isn't a journey you can make alone. For egos only become persons in relationships of love and friendship, and not only is there within us a deep human instinct to belong, but the whole impetus of Jesus' teaching is towards the creating of community, and St Paul's teaching, and the whole New Testament story most powerfully witnesses to this truth: that what every church exists to do is to bring us into the Kingdom – damaged, dysfunctional people that we are – and recreate us as the Body of Christ in the new creation that exists since that first Easter Day.

Now every community needs a base, and from the start Christians have set aside buildings where the church can come together to do certain things which are essential to their journey: to hear the word of God proclaimed, to celebrate that story of God's self-giving love, the story of a birth and a life and a death and a rising which contains and unites and illuminates our own human stories of living and suffering and dying and makes sense of them. When each of us comes to look back in the evening of our lives at what is for us of lasting value, I guess we shall remember certain people and certain places with particular affection. The place, perhaps, in which you or your children were baptized or confirmed or married, or where those you have loved most have been brought for their funeral.

The Bible, after all, has a very sacramental view of place: the belief that we encounter God in this or that specific place in order that we may consequently find him everywhere. The God of both the Old and the New Testament is one who tabernacles with his people on Mount Sinai, at Bethel and Shiloh and in the Temple. And the scandal of the gospel is the incarnation: God made known in the life and death of a crucified Jew from the unimportant town of Nazareth. Canterbury and Mount Athos, Iona and Lindisfarne, Jerusalem and Zagorsk – these are the grand places of God's epiphany, and yet some of us may find God in more modest places of worship. For just as houses pick up the spirit of those who live in them, so churches soak up into themselves the vibrations of the people who have prayed and grieved so fiercely within their walls, and the stones begin to absorb something of the beauty of the worship and the human longings that have filled the air.

Yet God's building is not primarily in terms of public edifices in brick and wood and glass and stone, but flesh: living stones, in St Peter's words, whose foundation stone is Jesus Christ. And we who have given our allegiance to Christ are called to live as those who have harmonized their public and their private journeys, so that there is an integrity between what we do and what we are, between how we live and what we believe.

We are to 'stand by those truths' we have learned and are assured of. For even in this rapidly changing world there are truths which anchor us to the reality who is God. This is not a plea for some sort of frightening fundamentalism. It is not a frightening fundamentalism, but divine mercy which the Christian Church exists to preach. When Solomon builds his great temple in Jerusalem and dedicates it to God, the Lord says: 'I have hallowed this house, which thou hast built, to put my name there for ever; and mine eyes and my heart shall be there perpetually.'

The truth we have learned and are assured of as the Body of Christ is that God's name is Father and his heart is a heart of love. So that, in the words of St John of the Cross, 'When the evening of our life comes, we shall be judged on love': judged on whether what we believe matches how we live. But we shall be judged too on whether by our sensitive response we have helped men and women who come to us searching for divine mercy become aware that God's name is Father and that his heart is a heart of love.

There will be among them those whose lives have been badly bruised, who may come in desperation and without hope. And perhaps we shall be judged most of all on whether we make it easy for them to come to our places of worship and find not only the beauty of stone and glass and music and liturgy, but truthful words and caring people, and so go out encouraged, strengthened, consoled and affirmed.

6

A Disturbing and Disruptive Figure

Comfort, comfort ye my people, says your God. Isaiah 40.1

'Who are you?' they asked. 'You who live like some roughly dressed vagrant in the desert. What do you want of us? You challenge us to repent, but we find you a disturbing and disruptive figure.' As disturbing and disruptive, no doubt, as all those others who have claimed special insights into truth: some of them authentic, true men and women of God, but many of them quite bizarre – for there is a thin line between the prophet and the fanatic. The prophet is one who discerns the signs of the times and by standing against the grain of popular opinion points to truths the rest of us miss. The fanatic is like the man who walked up and down Oxford Street for years with a billboard saying that God wants us all to eat lentils and sultanas.

And so they press John the Baptist for an answer. 'Who are you? Why should we listen to you?'

John's reply is to draw on that most profound and lyrical of Jewish prophets, the one known as Second Isaiah, the one who hundreds of years earlier had spoken to the Jewish refugees exiled in Babylon, and assured them that God was ready to restore them and bring them home. John quotes the familiar words: 'Comfort, comfort ye my people, says your God', and which go on, 'a voice cries: in the wilderness prepare the way of the LORD, make straight in the desert a highway for our God.'

'You know Isaiah's words,' says John. 'I am their fulfilment. I am that voice crying in the wilderness, warning you, urging you to repent and so prepare yourself, for God is about to reveal himself to you in a new and decisive way.'

In an Advent collect we ask God to inspire 'the ministers and stewards of your truth so that, like John the Baptist, they may

16

turn our disobedient hearts to the law of love.' And what I learn from Second Isaiah and John the Baptist is that it is not enough to think of God in terms of a loving and benevolent and ever-forgiving creator, for that is to view him one-eyed, to ignore the unimaginable space between him and us, which only he could cross – that is to be blind to the awesome nature of his glory, his majesty and his holiness.

What makes that passage of Isaiah so striking is his aware-ness of *both* aspects of God: his otherness and his nearness. On the one hand, his unimaginable beauty and power: 'Every valley shall be lifted up, and every mountain and hill shall be made low . . . the glory of the LORD shall be revealed, and all flesh shall see it together. Behold, the LORD God comes with might.' Majestic, triumphalist language: God the creator who holds the whole world in his hand.

But then, in the very next breath, comes the astonishing: 'He will feed his flock as a shepherd, he will gather the lambs in his arms, he will carry them in his bosom, and gently lead those that are with young.'

This is the God who speaks 'tenderly to Jerusalem . . . that her iniquity is pardoned'; and these are the words Jesus too will take from Isaiah and apply to himself when he says that he is the Good Shepherd searching at great cost for those who are lost.

Now it is this dual, two-eyed vision of the majesty and com-passion of God which we who are 'ministers and stewards of the truth' are to proclaim: his judgement, which after Good Friday can never be separated from his mercy. Like John the Baptist we who dare to stand in pulpits and speak of what is holy and mys-terious must always point away from ourselves and say: 'Don't look at me! Look beyond me to the God in whom we all live and move and have our being, and yet who was once uniquely revealed in Jesus Christ.'

Like John we have to say, 'There stands one among you (per-haps still unrecognized by you) and I am not fit to undo his sandal-strap.' That was the most menial service performed by a slave who had no status and no rights. John could think of no more powerful example to indicate his own insignificance compared with the greatness of God's Messiah. Yet later on, the one to whom he pointed was to kneel before his own disciples, undo their sandal-straps and wash their dusty feet, and by that last startling action showed how the majesty and compassion of God are in him mysteriously combined. It would have astonished John the Baptist. It astonished the disciples. It will seem to us both amazing yet entirely natural once we see how here, in Jesus Christ, the two aspects of God – his power and his love – are most wonderfully combined.

Here is a God who shows the nature of his majesty by humbly kneeling at our feet. For that is what love always does when faced with human need. And it is that proper love, that Christlike love, which should reduce us to a wondering silence, and by which one day we shall ourselves be judged.

7

With Astonishment and Wonder

When the Lord comes, he will bring to light things hidden in darkness.
1 Corinthians 4.5

In an Advent collect we ask God to strengthen 'the ministers and stewards of thy mysteries' and St Paul writes of himself as 'a steward of the mysteries of God.' He goes on to say that 'when the Lord comes, he will bring to light things hidden in darkness'. There are aspects of God, of the Christian gospel, and indeed of life itself, that are mysterious and will remain mysterious until that unimaginable day when we no longer see through a glass darkly but, with astonishment and wonder, face to face.

Yet 'mystery' is a word that needs rather careful unpacking. 'The highest knowledge', wrote Albert Schweitzer, 'is to know we are surrounded by mystery', and Pascal once said, 'I am astonished at the boldness with which people undertake to speak of God.'

We may want it clear and simple, but it's not, and ultimately everything is mystery. I am a mystery and so are you. Human life and birth and death are a mystery, as are suffering and human compassion and love. And so is every leaf and flower and fern and every garden slug. And the religious person in the broadest sense is the one who looks on the mystery of all living things, and the mystery that lies beyond and behind and within them – the mystery of God – and is filled with awe.

Now 'mystery' in this sense is not something to be discovered by human reasoning – as in some Agatha Christie or P. D. James murder mystery – or even one day to be fully understood as scientists increase the boundaries of knowledge. For by 'the mysteries of God' St Paul means two things: he means that which is beyond our comprehension and always will be, and that which has to do with the hidden things of the spirit rather than what we can see and touch and analyse. But he also means truths which God has chosen to reveal at particular times and through particular people: secrets which God has disclosed to those with eyes to see.

And for the New Testament the central mystery, the great act of divine disclosure, is the mystery of Christ – the fact that, for those with eyes to see – here is the human face of God. Here is the mystery that those who are 'stewards of the mysteries of God' have to preach – that God was once present in human shape, yet only recognized by the eye of faith – that in order to show his power and glory and God-likeness he chooses to reveal himself in a man who kneels, servant-like, to wash his disciples' feet, and later on is hanged, like some common criminal, on a cross; and that in order to reveal eternal truths he chooses time, and in order to reveal his Spirit he chooses flesh.

Jesus himself uses the word 'mystery'; he talks of the mystery of the Kingdom of God that is beginning to be revealed in his words and actions. And when John the Baptist sends to ask if Jesus is truly the Messiah, the Christ, Jesus points him to the unmistakable signs: the blind receive their sight, the lame walk, the lepers are cleansed, the deaf hear, the dead are raised up, and the poor have the gospel preached to them. Yet here, too, is mystery. For some recognize in these signs the Christ, the Saviour, while others see but fail to understand. And in order to reveal the mystery of the new life he offers us, Christ chooses the fallible, broken body of the Church. In order to make his living presence known to all ages, he chooses the bread and wine of the Eucharist that we sometimes call 'the Holy mysteries.' And, most mysterious of all, to speak of the mysteries of God he uses the poor stammerings of those who stand in pulpits.

There are, in *King Lear*, two marvellous lines which the dying Lear speaks as he holds the dead Cordelia in his arms: We are those, he says, who must 'take upon us the mystery of things as if we were God's spies.' What does that mean in terms of *our* ministry: and I speak not just of those of us who are ordained, but the ministry of all baptized, believing Christians who take their faith seriously?

I suggest it means this. Many today feel bewildered and confused – hurt and anxious and isolated and unloved – perhaps unforgiving and unforgiven. Sometimes we may feel all those things ourselves. Yet faith means trusting that Christ was the authentic revelation of God, and that in his living and dying and rising he unlocked some of the mysteries of how God brings good out of evil, and how irreplaceable and precious each one of us is in God's sight. Perhaps there has been someone in your life who has helped make sense of some of its mysteries for you, someone perhaps who has wrestled with the mystery of bereavement in the light Christ gives, or who, by the quality of their listening, or the courage with which they have faced suffering, or by small acts of kindness and encouragement, have given you glimpses of the love of the Christlike God. That is what we are called to do for each other.

For one thing is sure. Ultimately the gospel will be credible to the world only if the world sees evidence of a quality of life in the Church which it cannot find elsewhere. Being a steward of the mysteries of God means trying to live our lives as individuals, and as the Body of Christ, in ways that are hard to account for if the God made known in Jesus is not at their centre: lives which, often feebly, but in the end unmistakably, point, as John the Baptist did, to the Christ, and through him to the Father of us all.

8

The Silence of Our Full Attention

Silence, all mankind, in the presence of the LORD; for he has bestirred
himself out of his holy dwelling place. Zechariah 2.13

I suspect that most clergy have recurring dreams, almost certainly anxiety dreams. Mine take one of two forms. In the first
I am standing at the altar about to celebrate the Eucharist and I
can't find the right page. Every page I turn to is either blank or
in Double Dutch. In the second dream I am standing at the pulpit about to preach, and I open and shut my mouth but nothing
comes out, for I have lost my notes and my mind is blank and I
am speechless and ill-prepared and have nothing to say.

All our words are, in the end, fragile – imprecise and ephemeral and approximate. In the face of pain and grief all our words
ultimately prove inadequate. It was Flaubert who wrote that in
the face of suffering and dying, 'human language is like a kettle
on which we beat out tunes for bears to dance to, when all the
time we are longing to move the stars to pity.' There are times
when what we need are not words but a human touch, a hug, a
presence of someone beside us and on our side.

Of course, all our words prove hopelessly inadequate in trying
to describe the mystery of the all-holy and indescribable God. In
particular, the latter days of Advent leading to Christmas call not
so much for words, but silence.

'Silence, all mankind, in the presence of the LORD', writes
Zechariah; 'for he has bestirred himself out of his holy dwelling place.' 'The Virgin is with child', we understand in Advent,
'and will soon give birth to a son, and she will call his name
Emmanuel: God with us.'

It is precisely at that point where we stand empty, speechless,
without any words left, uninspired and needing grace, that God

acts. He takes the initiative and comes among us. It isn't in any words of ours but in silence and in stillness that we shall catch the beat of angels' wings and be brought to kneel before the wonder of all wonders – a baby in a crib who is the Word made flesh.

On Christmas Eve night a million churches all over the world are crammed to the doors with people gathered in silence to celebrate this most ordinary, yet extraordinary, act of grace, a child is born in the dark among the beasts, and things can never be the same again. For here is God acting once in history in a way that must fill us with wonder, cut through all our chatter, and reduce us to silence and bring us to our knees.

The Word is made flesh. The Word, that which most perfectly expresses the nature of God, is revealed in the only terms we can begin to understand: in human terms, God living our life and speaking our language. Ultimate Mystery is born with a skull you could crush one-handed. The creative and all-powerful Word is reduced to a child who must learn his first halting words at his mother's knee. God with us: a human touch, a hug, a presence of someone beside us and on our side.

Such a mystery must reduce us to silence. For only in silence, the silence of our full attention, can such a truth begin to be heard, such an act of grace begin to be understood. In silence. Or, perhaps, in music. Silence or music.

What need of words, then, as Christmas draws so close? Except those words of warning that cut through our talkative lives and say: 'Be still!' 'Be silent, all mankind, in the presence of the LORD!' Stop your busy-ness. Give attention to God and what he is seeking to tell us of himself. He would have us know that he is Christlike. He would have our full attention as Christmas comes, that we may avoid being nostalgic for the past, or anxious for the future, and give our life in this present moment back to God by responding to his grace in the birth of Jesus Christ.

9

A Very Remarkable Mother

And Mary said: Let it be to me according to your word. Luke 1.38

I want to think a little about Mary and her significance for us, but first I want to reflect on what happens in a million churches all over the world on Christmas Eve and Christmas morning. People gather to celebrate that most ordinary and extraordinary of events, the birth of a child. God acts once in history in a way so simple and so direct and so startling that we are stopped short and for once reduced to silence. For here is an event which changes everything, an event utterly unexpected and unpredictable, a baby in a wooden manger who by the time he hangs on his wooden cross will have so illuminated the nature of God and of human life that it is as if a great blazing torch has been set in the world to lighten our darkness and warm our hearts.

What a mystery it is! That God – the mysterious, unimaginable maker of all things – should allow us a glimpse of himself in the only terms we can possibly understand: that he should make himself known in human terms as love, and in Jesus speak to our lives at their deepest and most vulnerable point. His name: Emmanuel, God-is-with-us. The Word made flesh. The Word who lying in Mary's arms cannot actually speak a word – and a mystery such as that must surely silence us. For only in silence, the silence that grows out of the giving of our full attention, can such a truth begin to be heard and understood.

What need of words, then, as Christmas draws so close? Except those words of warning that cut through our talkative lives and say: 'For once, be still. Be silent, all mankind, before the LORD!' Stop your busy-ness. Give attention to God and what he is seeking to tell you of himself. He would have us know that he is Christlike. He would have our full attention as Christmas comes once again, that we may stop dreaming about the past, or worrying about the future, and give this present moment in which we live wholly to him by responding to his amazing grace in Jesus Christ.

Listen to these beautiful words of an anonymous medieval poem.

> I sing of a maiden
> That is matchless;
> King of all kings
> For her son she chose.
>
> He came all so still
> Where his mother was,
> As dew in April
> That falleth on the grass.
>
> He came all so still
> To his mother's bower,
> As dew in April
> That falleth on the flower.
>
> He came all so still
> Where his mother lay,
> As dew in April
> That falleth on the spray.
>
> Mother and maiden
> Was never none but she;
> Well may such a lady
> God's mother be.

These words in honour of Mary are not much reflected in sub-sequent Anglican worship. While the Orthodox and Roman Catholic Churches have exalted the Virgin Mary to a position little short of the Godhead, the Church of England's approach to her has been very low key and pianissimo. And somewhat ambivalent. Yet she is the Queen of Saints, with more churches dedicated to her than to anyone else.

On Christmas Day, the theme is Jesus Christ, a human baby born of a human mother, who as he grew mysteriously made God known in a unique way. But in the days leading up to Christmas the Church's theme is the annunciation, the story of Gabriel appearing to Mary and telling her she will have a child, and we are encouraged to think about the woman who made the incarnation possible. For so much of the world's joy hangs on the slender thread of Mary's response. It isn't simply that she made the incarnation possible by her 'Yes', by her bewildered assent, 'be it unto me according to your word'. She is not honoured just because she gave birth to Jesus. No, she made the incarnation possible and she is honoured and loved because she was his *mother*, with everything that word implies.

Now it isn't hard to find books and articles in theological journals about the importance of Mary as the one who supplies our need for the feminine in the Godhead, or about her effectiveness in countering the over-masculine nature of Protestant theology. And that may be all very interesting – well, fairly interesting – but somehow it doesn't touch the heart. Indeed, it tends to dehumanize Mary who has a claim on our love and devotion because, as the mother of Jesus, she did for him what no one else could have done.

I was once in a group who were talking about a man whose integrity and singleness of purpose and very practical goodness had impressed us all. When we had finished discussing him an elderly woman who had remained silent said: 'Well, he must have had a very remarkable mother.'

And that seems to me to go to the heart of an aspect of the incarnation we don't often think about, the effect on Jesus of his mother. His parents, if you like, for it is to our parents that we owe a good deal of how our character has been formed, and yet it is a mother who often plays the most formative part. It's very often from her that we learn to love. For our ability to love, to look beyond ourselves, first as tiny babies to one other person, and later to lots of people – this ability depends on the kind of love we receive when we are very young.

Somehow a mother must walk that knife-edge between giving her child security and letting him or her go free. She knows she cannot possess her child for ever and if she is wise she will delight to see the ability to give love developing in her growing child, and stimulate and encourage it. And so the most crucial test of a mother's relationship with her child is whether she can give that child a sense of her non-possessive yet unconditional love, so that he or she can break away from her for increasingly long periods and find proper freedom and independence.

Mary was the first person to love Jesus and the first person he loved, and we honour her because she taught him the meaning of love. I don't mean simply that she loved him. I mean she taught him the language of love: taught him by her own example that love must be generous, unselfish, non-possessive, and always in the end costly. Certainly Mary (who had been warned of the sword that would pierce her heart) found it hard and once or twice she remonstrated with her son: once when he was a child in the Temple, once at a wedding feast, and once when he was exhausting himself with the crowds. But she listened when he explained how he must be about his Father's business, and she pondered these things in her heart, and she let him go. She freed him for his own vocation and we hear no more of her until the day when she stands at the foot of his cross.

Christmas points us to the mystery of the incarnation, of 'the love that moves the sun and the other stars' once made known in Jesus Christ. Part of that mystery is the role God entrusts to Mary as she teaches her son the language of love. And so as Christmas comes again, think about this extraordinary truth: that God can make himself known only with our consent and co-operation. He is as dependent on us as a child is dependent on its mother. His will to make his love known in his world is no more than a dream unless people like us say 'Yes.' '*Yes*, I accept that love is generous and not self-seeking, that it is costly and may lead to the foot of the cross. I accept that is the way of life I have chosen.'

Each time we can even in a small way say 'Yes' in that sense we are living in the spirit of Mary as well as in the spirit of Jesus, and Word is being made flesh over and over again, but now in *our* words and through *our* lives, for now there is no other way.

Part 2

Christmas

10

A Restless Hunger for God

No-one has ever seen God; it is the only Son, who is nearest to the Father's heart, who has made him known. John 1.18

It can be a dark place, this world of ours. Which of us does not know times of darkness in our own lives? Times of sickness or of grief, times of depression and perhaps despair. Days and nights when God seems distant and remote.

Yet we Christians gather on Christmas Eve in our millions in churches bathed in light. What do we hope to find? A Christmas crib? Talk of a birth, of a child in a manger, or angels and shepherds? How can that change anything?

It can't, unless in the birth of Jesus we sense the reality, the power of a light which can never be quenched. Unless we see in our mind's eye a great company of people from every nation upon earth like us drawn together by a restless hunger for God, drawn by this child who was to claim to be the light of the world, and who illuminates once and for all time the true nature of God and the true purpose of man.

He too was born into a cruel and violent world, a place of darkness and full of shadows, of pain and sudden death. The child who was laid in a wooden manger was one day to hang on a wooden cross. Yet between that birth at Bethlehem and that death at Calvary we witness a life so full of grace and truth and love, so open to God, that the one who was closest to him and knew him best of all could later write: 'No-one has ever seen God; it is the only Son, who is nearest to the Father's heart, who has made him known.'

At Christmas we celebrate that birth. However dimly, however fragile our faith, we can glimpse just a little that here is a man unlike any other, a man who with absolute authority assures us that we are created and held by – and always will be held by – a

God who loves and values us beyond our imagining. At this most holy of times we can glimpse too the possibility of that new life, which he calls the Kingdom of God, where justice and mercy go hand in hand and the peoples of the world live together in love and peace.

'The light shines in the dark, writes St John, 'and the darkness cannot quench it.'

Now I don't know what form the darkness may take for you. But I do know this. If you can see beyond the trimmings of Christmas, beyond the child in the manger and stories of the shepherds and angels, if you can trust that in Jesus Christ God speaks in a human life, then perhaps you will come to see that there is a reality deeper and more lasting than all our experience of darkness and pain and loss, that the light that shines at Christmas is the fatherly love of God spelled out in the only terms we can understand.

You cannot prove it beyond any shadow of doubt. But for 2,000 years people like us have accepted on trust that it is true – that God is with us, that God is made known in Jesus – and it has changed their lives.

Love was made flesh at Christmas, and love is made flesh again and again and again, whenever you and I turn to Jesus Christ, and allow him to be born in us and take possession of our hearts.

Christ Our Light

The light shines on in the dark, and the darkness has never quenched it.
John 1.5

It was at night, in the dark, that Jesus was born, and a brilliant
star, so they say, stood over Bethlehem. Each of us must sometimes know what it is like to lie awake in the dark, longing for
the dawn. But for many the dawn, when it comes, doesn't put an
end to the darkness.

It may be the darkness of a sudden and terrible loss, the darkness of bewilderment and grief. Or the darkness, perhaps, of the
hospital bed or the terminal illness. Or it may be the darkness of
inner fears and anxieties.

These are dark powers which are so pervasive we can never
fully escape or avoid them. And yet what the birth of Jesus says
is that they do not have the final word. What Christmas comes to
tell us is that it is possible not to be dragged down and destroyed
by such forces of darkness, but to choose the light and to trust
the light: to choose to dwell, come what may, in the house of
love.

On Christmas Eve all over the world cathedrals and churches
are ablaze with lights which challenge the dark. On Christmas
Eve, whose dawn brings Christmas Day, a million candles burn
at a million Midnight Masses, not just to give illumination, but
to speak of the truth proclaimed by St John when, speaking of
Christ, he says: 'The light shines on in the dark, and the darkness
has never quenched it.'

It is an unlikely truth, heaven knows, yet it is a truth that in
our own time, as in past times, men and women have lived and
died for. I once received a Christmas card which read:

One simple woman and her child
Revealed such glory
That the cold, silent darkness
Was for ever broken,
For God had spoken.

Christmas comes to remind us that there has lived a man in whose life there was *no* darkness. A man who was wholly light, because his life was so open to God and his neighbour, so full of grace and truth, that he reveals for all time truths we could not otherwise have guessed. That is to say, here in this man is the truth about God; God is Christlike, compassionate, tender-hearted and forgiving, not against us in earthquake or sickness or disaster or death, but with us, suffering with us and loving us to the end. Why are we so resistant to that truth? Why do we still associate God with the power of darkness?

Here in this man is the truth about each one of us, the truth we know instinctively in our hearts and which we celebrate at Christmas. The truth that we too are made in the likeness of God: made to love and not to hate, to give and not to grasp, to heal and not destroy.

Now it's not hard to see that when light shines in darkness the darkness will try to extinguish it, and sometimes it seems to have succeeded. On the cross the one who had said he was the light of the world seemed to be quenched like a doused candle. But it was not so, for love is not so easily killed. And each year, in the darkness of that other memorable night, Easter Eve, we light the Easter candle to assert the triumph of the light and sing aloud, 'Christ our light!' And we do so because the child born at Christmas was to show by his death that there is something even more powerful than the grave, and that is the power of God to hold in being you – me – souls he has created to know him and be with him for ever.

'The light shines in the darkness, and the darkness has not quenched it.' I don't know what form the darkness may take for you at Christmas. But I do know this. If you can see beyond the crib and the candles and the angels and stories of shepherds and wise men, if you can recognize that child for who he is and trust the man he became, then he will lead you to God. The God who speaks our language: the language of human love and human suffering. And then you will learn – perhaps for the first time, perhaps simply more deeply than ever before – that the darkness of human pain and loss is no less real, but that it is illuminated and ultimately transformed by the light of the steadfast love of God.

One simple woman and her child
Revealed such glory
That the cold, silent darkness
Was for ever broken.
For God has spoken.

God has spoken. And in Jesus Christ, his Word made flesh, he invites us to trust him and choose to dwell in the house of love.

12

Beautifully Simple and Strangely Mysterious

And the Word became flesh. John 1.14

If I were to ask, 'What draws you to church at Christmas?' I guess I should get myriad different answers. Some are drawn because they believe that love came down at Christmas and are grateful. Some because they would like to believe and are searching. Some because they are hurt and need consoling. Some because something – the silence, perhaps, or the holiness of the sacred space, or the old familiar carols – resonates in the deep places of their mind and spirit and meets a kind of hunger which nothing else satisfies in the same way.

But I believe that in all our varied motives for being here tonight there is a common thread. Call it a kind of homesickness for the wholeness that eludes us: a yearning for the answer to the mystery of our lives. Call it a hunger for God. Call it my need to know in this dark, threatening world that I matter, and that I am loved.

Christmas comes to remind us of a truth that has the power to transform our lives. It speaks of a birth and of a life like ours, and yet unlike. For the man this child of Bethlehem became shows us God. Not God in all his unimaginable power and majesty, but God revealing himself in the only terms in which we can recognize or understand him – in our terms – in terms of a baby at his mother's breast, a man who heals and forgives and loves and consoles and encourages those he meets: a man who washes his friends' feet and breaks bread with them, who dies in agony on a cross and whom death cannot hold. This man gives God a human face. And what Christmas proclaims is at once beautifully simple and strangely mysterious. It is this: God is Christlike, vulnerable, not (as it so often feels) against us and indifferent to our needs. The God of Jesus Christ, the God *revealed* in Jesus Christ, is on our side, loving us and valuing us more than we can conceive. Emmanuel: God with us.

It is because I believe deep within myself that this is so that I dare invite you to respond afresh to this great mystery, to take comfort and know again the wonder and the hope of the Word made flesh: God made man in Jesus.

13

Consoled and Encouraged

'And they shall name him Emmanuel, which means, "God is with us."'
Matthew 1.23

All good stories begin: 'Once upon a time.' And the child in us all begins to listen. We want to know what's coming next and how the story ends. For all good stories have a meaning; and all the best stories contain a truth which can illuminate, or even change your life.

There has never been a better story than the one the Church tells at Christmas. It begins: 'Once upon a time a child was born in a remote town, in darkness and among the beasts.' And the story ends: 'And nothing can ever be the same again.'

The story begins with a birth and it goes on to tell of a man who taught, and healed people, and served and loved them, and suffered and was killed. Yet the story ends not with a cross but in the Easter garden.

What this story says is that 'once upon a time', at one precise moment of human history, the invisible God revealed himself in human terms, for they are the only terms we can understand. And the meaning of this story lies in one of the names they give to the child: Emmanuel. For it means God-is-with-us. God is on our side: God living our life and speaking our language.

It is of course a love story: the story of the love between God and us. It's a story about seeing the human face of God so that, just for a little while, as the story is told again at Christmas, it reduces us to silence. Once upon a time, we hear, a child was born and we become still, and some spirit, some hope, some deep yearning for God, is born again into our cynical, violent and restless world of which we are a part, and which makes such desperate claims upon our lives.

If you journey to the church at Christmas it is, I guess, because you believe the story – or because there is that deep within you that would like to believe it. Perhaps you realize that these words about a star and a stable and a child are not mere words written on sand, but poetry that points beyond itself to the very heart of reality. And once you have grasped the meaning of this story nothing is ever quite the same again.

It's not easy to speak to a staggeringly diverse audience. There are some whose lives seem uncomplicated and brimful of happiness. But there will be many others who bear scars and hurts of many kinds and wish to be consoled and encouraged on what is often a tough and lonely journey, and sometimes a difficult time of year. What I would say to each unique one of you is this: let the Christmas story speak afresh to you both of God's love for you and of your value to him.

Someone wrote to me once to say thank you because I had counselled her during a time of crisis and depression. And she wrote, 'The thing that brought me through was the relief of knowing that you were not on the other side: you were on *my* side sitting beside me, understanding and sharing my pain.' That's the meaning of this story too – God-with-us, not against us – not remote or indifferent as he sometimes may seem, but on our side, loving us and understanding and sharing both our good times and our bad: the Christlike God, the down-to-earth God, who once upon a time made himself known at Bethlehem in terms we can understand, and took us by the hand so that he might lead us home.

14

The Human Face of God

In him was life, and that life was the light of men. The light shines in the
dark, and the darkness has not overcome it. John 1.4–6

There once was an unusual advertisement in the *Guardian*. It was
an appeal for Bosnian refugees. It took the form of a blank page
on which there was a small notice that simply read: 'Please don't
make us have to fill this space with pictures of dying children.'

In other words: you already know the facts; you've already
seen the pictures. Follow your heart and let the deep human
instinct for compassion move you now to action, and you will
be taking a small stand against the dark and opting for the light.

Now I don't intend to fill *this* space with descriptions of dying
children or the world's violence or the darkness of economic
uncertainty, unemployment and homelessness. But yet I would
not dare to preach the gospel at all unless I knew that there is
an unchanging source of hope and light even at the heart of the
darkness. We speak as if the darkness is greater now than it once
was. I don't believe it for a moment. All that's changed is the
power of the media to show us human wickedness and pain with
a startling force and immediacy.

For Jesus was born into a world that was equally dark, cruel
and violent: a world of slavery and foreign occupation, of torture
and injustice, where after a rigged trial a man could die slowly and
painfully having been nailed to a wooden cross. And those who
first told the Christmas story knew exactly what they were doing
in contrasting darkness and light, evil and good, despair and hope,
when they wrote of a star and a birth by lamplight in a stable at
night, where the source of the world's true light is astonishingly
enclosed within the circle of a girl's arms. As St John puts it: 'In
him was life, and that life was the light of men. The light shines in
the dark, and the darkness has not overcome it.'

I can well remember holding within the circle of my arms a very powerful sign of hope, my newborn grandchild, Anna, and I was awed by the thought of all the potential packed in that tiny body, the power she would one day have for good or evil, the power we all have to help create light or to collude with darkness.

Then I think of that other baby, and of how his life was to change the life of millions and prove a great beacon of light set in the world to show us how we can live surrounded by darkness and not be overcome by it.

At Christmas we gather as men and women who believe that in this child and the man he became we see the human face of God. We believe that here in Jesus, God is saying in language we can understand that he is with us, on our side, one with us in our living and our dying. We believe he is the Christlike God, as loving and forgiving and compassionate as Jesus Christ was. And we believe that when we respond to others with instinctive acts of kindness and compassion, we are being most authentically human, most truly ourselves: most like him.

To celebrate Christmas, then, is to refuse to let ourselves be dragged down by the surrounding darkness. It is to renew our hope and our trust in the God revealed in Jesus Christ, the light that shines in the darkness and which that darkness will not and cannot overcome.

15

Hope

'And they shall name him Emmanuel, which means, "God is with us."'
Matthew 1.23

Many of us can remember when Brian Keenan, John McCarthy and Terry Waite were held hostage. Three men who lost their liberty but not their freedom. For even when life was reduced to a grubby space six foot by four, even when chained to a wall in a dark and claustrophobic cell, they never lost hope. The hope that they had a future, the belief that things would change, a dogged expectancy when things were at their most hopeless that in the end good would prove more powerful than evil. And once again, in the hostages, the strength of the human spirit in adversity was shown to be quite extraordinary.

While I served as Dean of Westminster we put on regular supper parties for those with the AIDS virus and their carers. While talking with a young man who was HIV positive, I asked him what he thought the churches could provide in a dark time. Without a moment's hesitation he replied with the one word: 'Hope.'

What he was asking for was, I suggest, something that goes even deeper than the hope of the hostages. Their hope was largely drawn from a strength they found deep within themselves, a stubborn refusal to submit to darkness and despair. But the hope of which the New Testament speaks is not based on our own inner courage or resilience, but on something even more remarkable: it is rooted in what God did once in Jesus Christ. Hope is a story that begins: Once upon a time a child was born, in darkness and insecurity, into a cruel and violent world; and because of that child and the man he became, nothing can ever be quite the same again. Those who tell his story call him Emmanuel, hoping we will grasp the full implications of that word, for it means 'God is with us.' God is the life-giving creative Spirit, once made known in Jesus, who is with us at every point in our lives. He is on our side, sharing our lives and speaking our language. And he is the God of hope.

My hope is that this is true. In other words, this is my faith, a truth that I am prepared to trust beyond all other truths. I don't say that lightly. Only a fool would claim that hope or faith – and they go hand in hand – are cheaply come by. Yet my hope has nothing to do with wishful thinking or blinkered sight. Priests are not blind or addlepated (well, not many of them anyway). We too face and share the darkness of human life. And yet, at Christmas we claim that there is a truth revealed in this birth, this life and this death deeper and more persuasive than all the world's darkness.

It is a truth that says: to hope is to keep faith with what Jesus Christ revealed of what a human being truly is. To hope is to keep faith with the deep, instinctive God-given and Godlike compassion we feel within us in the face of human need. To hope is to refuse to let ourselves be demoralized, sucked down into the all-too-evident darkness. To hope is to believe that no one – yes, no one – is beyond redemption.

Finally, to hope is to stand with that great number of men and women who gather in churches in every nation upon earth at Christmas because they believe – or perhaps long to believe – the witness of this Christ-child who, alone of all our race, was to grow to look at the face of the transcendent mystery and say that his name was Father. 'Whoever has seen me,' he said (my anguish and suffering, my love, my forgiveness, my compassion), 'has seen the Father.'

Our hope is, literally, Jesus Christ. And to celebrate Christmas is to renew our trust in the God he reveals: the one true light that shines in the darkness and which that darkness has not and can never overcome.

16

All We Need to Know

And the Word became flesh and lived among us. John 1.14

In Westminster Abbey lie the ashes of Thomas Hardy, novelist and poet. Would he, I wonder, when alive, have attended services at Christmas? Certainly he rejected any formal Christian belief. Yet I think he might have attended, for he was a regretful unbeliever who often went to church. You can't be a great novelist and not be aware of the human mystery, and few have written more profoundly of human hopes and fears, or of our homesickness for a world transformed by the forces of good and the power of love.

Churches fill at Christmas, some having come because they believe that the unimaginable God *was* once made visible man in Palestine: and some because they half-believe or would like to believe it, drawn, in Hardy's words, 'Hoping it may be so.' For there is a strange power in the familiar words of the Christmas story and the carols, that draws us at Christmas and meets a kind of hunger in us which is in fact a hunger for God. For of one thing I am sure. Wherever we are on our human journey we all have this in common – a need to be noticed, to be valued and affirmed – a need to know that we matter and that we are loved.

It's at once very hard and very easy to speak of the meaning of Christmas. For how can any words of mine hope to unwrap the mystery of God's action? And yet there is an utterly simple gift at the heart of it: a gift to which the child lying in the manger points. He isn't the gift, he is just the form in which the gift comes.

For consider: at Christmas all of us, except the very poor and unusually mean, will give and receive presents. Some will delight us. Others may make us groan. But there will be one or two gifts that have a deeper significance, for a gift chosen with special care is the best way I can say to you: 'I love you. You matter to me more than you will ever know.' 'Thank you', you say, unwrapping it. 'But you shouldn't have.' 'Oh, it's nothing', I reply. But it's not nothing: it's everything. It's a tangible expression of how much you matter to me. And just as nothing in the world is more painful than loving and knowing that we are not loved in return, so nothing fulfils us as loving someone and knowing beyond a shadow of a doubt that we are loved in return.

Now I'd be hard pressed to remember more than a handful of things my wife and I have given to each other over the years. What I know beyond doubt is that the presents we have exchanged are the way we have affirmed our love; for the true gift is our relationship. And that's why the child in the manger and the man he became are not in themselves God's gift to us, but simply the means he has chosen to show us how much he values each one of us. The true gift is our relationship with God, which on his part is a relationship of love. He will love us throughout our lives and in and beyond our deaths. He can't help it: it's his nature. And nothing less than that is what God is affirming in the birth and life and death and rising of Jesus Christ.

And so we come, the believing and the half-believing, and hear once more the familiar words, hoping it may be so. If I say, 'I give you my word', I mean that from my heart I say to you: 'It *is* so.' Here, now, in this holy season may we let the story of the birth of Jesus at whatever level we need to hear it speak to us of God's love for us and our unique value to him.

At Christmas it is God who says in Jesus: 'I give you my word, my word made flesh.' That, in the end, is all we need to know.

17

I Trust

Whoever has seen me has seen the Father. John 14.9

Words are fragile things. They are often imprecise, approximate, misleading. Poets handle them like jewels and polish them until they shine. Politicians may sometimes bend them, and dictators twist them, so that – like those of Humpty Dumpty in *Through the Looking-Glass, and What Alice Found There* – they mean what you want them to mean.

But if we are to communicate with one another, words are all we have. I may have the most beautiful thoughts about God, but unless I can put them into speech, unless I can give them flesh and incarnate them, you will have no chance of understanding those truths which are at my centre.

I must therefore choose my words with great care. I cannot pretend to things I don't believe, or indulge in that kind of religious talk which is just sound and fury, signifying nothing. I must speak only of what I know, for unless I give you something of myself I shan't be communicating with you except at the most trivial level.

Now this is not just the prologue to an address about Christmas. It goes at once to the very heart of it. For what is true of us is true of God, in whose likeness we are made, and who has chosen to reveal himself in the only terms we could begin to understand: in terms of flesh and blood – to make himself incarnate – to make himself vulnerable. The Word became flesh and stands revealed in human terms as a man who invites our response.

It is an awesome and astonishing thing that in the man Jesus God is made known, and yet (if God is love) what could be more natural than that the Creator should cut through all our human chatter and speculation and reveal himself in a birth so startling and a life so compelling that once we grasp what it means we are not so much provoked to speech as reduced to silence. For there is no other way God can communicate with us: no other way for Love to express itself. For love, even in our human terms, has to be made incarnate. A love that is not made flesh, not earthed in particular words and actions, is not really love at all, just an emotional feeling. In one way or another, love is always costly. It means giving of yourself, making yourself vulnerable, risking being misunderstood or rejected.

Only on the surface is Christmas the story of a stable, or shepherds and angels and a star: those are the words poets use to express their wonder that in this birth, in this child and in the man he became, God is made known, and he is made known as love. We mustn't let the trimmings of the Christmas story blind us to what the New Testament tells us about Jesus and what Jesus tells us about God.

What the New Testament tells us about Jesus is that he was a man whose every word and every action spoke of his knowledge of the Father, a man in whose presence the sick are healed and the sinful repent, a man who takes a towel and basin and washes his disciples' feet, a man who makes himself vulnerable even to the point of death, a man who, when nailed to a cross, forgives those who are nailing him there. In Jesus, love is made flesh. His words and actions are of a piece.

What then does Jesus tell us about God? He tells us that those who have seen him – given him their whole attention, really listened to his words and properly understood his actions – those who have done this have seen God. 'Whoever has seen me has seen the Father.' He says that they must come to know and trust God as their Father, believe that they are always in his presence, and understand that God is like one who watches and waits with infinite patience to run and fling his arms round the neck of his penitent child when he decides to come home.

Christmas Day, like Easter Day, or Pentecost, opens a window onto what is eternal and unchanging. For I guess we can only take in little by little, and in very simple human terms, the truth that God's love for us and our love for God is what will remain when all else is lost and left behind. And here we have it spelled out in terms of a baby at his mother's breast, a healing action, a forgiving word, a washing of feet, a breaking of bread, a cross and an empty grave.

What then does it mean to celebrate Christmas? It means believing that God has made himself known once in history – that he has, as it were, in Jesus a human face – and that in Jesus Christ God gives us his final and definitive word about himself and about ourselves, no matter how much clamour the world keeps up.

To celebrate Christmas is to say: I trust. Despite all the darkness, the pain and the evil of the world, despite the earthquake and the train crash and the air disaster, I trust that the love of God is the deepest, the most powerful reality of all. To celebrate Christmas is to say 'Amen' in the depth of our being to this word God has spoken, this word made flesh: to say 'Yes' to God's love made flesh, in Jesus Christ.

If Christmas Day is to transform every other day of the year then we need to come alive to the God who wants to be made flesh, not just once at Bethlehem, but in the life of every human being who will receive him. It is a slow business, a lifetime's pilgrimage, to build bridges of trust and love across the painful muddle of our lives. But it is only as we grow in that trust that we learn increasingly to look back at our life and recognize it as a place not of God's absence but of God's presence: God with us at every point, whether we recognize him or not, the Christlike God who searched us out at Bethlehem and took us by the hand so that he might bring us home.

18

The Nature of Love

And they shall name him Emmanuel, which means, 'God is with us.'
Matthew 1.23

Consider, first, the nature of love.

It must have been a joy to King Henry III that the very first people to be married in his new Abbey in 1269 were his son Edmund and his bride Aveline. To this day their bodies lie in two handsome tombs in Westminster Abbey.

No doubt they were in love. No doubt the spirit of what they had come to say 700 years ago was in essence what every husband says to his wife, and every wife to her husband, on their wedding day. 'Because I love you I want to share my life with you: I want to give you my heart.' Such love is costly and demanding but, when we achieve it, infinitely rewarding. But it isn't to be known or experienced chiefly in the words we say. It is recognized and nourished by our actions, by our care, our thoughtfulness, our readiness to forgive: above all, perhaps, by what I can only call the giving of proper attention the one to the other. For it is not on some Richter scale of passion or emotion that love is best defined; love is best defined by a life which is spent in the service of another, not protectively grasped but poured out and shared. Love may be quite often a kind of dying.

Consider, next, the nature of God. When I ask myself what for me matters most of all, what gives me existence and gives ultimate meaning to my life, I answer with the word 'God.' And in saying 'God' I am claiming that at the heart of creation I find an unfathomable mystery. But with the New Testament and the whole tradition of Christian belief I have to go on to say: 'And the deepest mystery of all is this, that in God sovereignty and compassion go hand in hand, and so he took upon himself the full weight of a human life and shared with us all the joys and all the pain of human living.'

The nature of love and the nature of God – the two come together and meet in a stable: a birth, a child and the man that child became – 'God with us.'

It is at once so breathtakingly simple that a child can respond to it. And it is so profoundly mysterious as to call from us a deep sense of wonder. And those who *truly* celebrate Christmas are those who have rediscovered in themselves that childlike sense of wonder and who are committed to so unlikely, so radical a belief, that either you must dismiss it or it will change your life. 'Love came down at Christmas.' God is love. Believe that, and it will change your whole understanding of God and of the world and of other people.

To believe in the child born once in Bethlehem is to believe also in the man that child became – the one who in his words and by his actions defines what love is, and what we are meant to be – the one whose life and death spell out the meaning of the steadfast love of God in the only language we can begin to understand.

This is the simple yet mysterious truth: what it means to be God is to pour yourself out in love, and those who were drawn to Jesus and followed him learned to know God in a new way: as the one in their midst, giving of himself for their sake. What we call the incarnation means that the words 'God', 'Jesus' and 'Love' belong together, and can never again be considered apart.

If that is so, should we not be dismayed by the world's pain and anguish, by the unimaginable suffering caused by an earthquake, a train crash or an air disaster, and do not those things make nonsense of the claim that God is love? Yes, we should be dismayed, for that very dismay is the form of love we call compassion. And no, it does not invalidate the Christmas truth, for right in the midst of such pain and suffering there are acts of courage and generosity and selflessness which reveal, for those with eyes to see, the face of Christ and the love of God in men and women. To celebrate Christmas is to say: I trust. Despite all the darkness and pain, despite accidents and natural disasters, I trust that the love of God is the deepest and most powerful reality of all. I trust in God's love made flesh in Jesus Christ.

Christmas Day, as it speaks of this ordinary but extraordinary birth, asserts that it is because you and I are made in Love's likeness, that Edmund's love for Aveline, and your love for your husband or wife or child or friend, and your compassion for someone in need, are literally Godlike. They have the divine character once the other person becomes as important to you as yourself, the focus of your full attention and therefore of your caring love.

Should we not be dismayed then by our frailty and our weakness and the shallowness of our loving, when marriages fail and friendships spoil and relationships go sour? Yes, we should be dismayed that we fall so short of what we might be. And no, we should not be discouraged, for what we seek is the most difficult and costly and worthwhile activity there could be. Human beings are weak and vacillating, which is why Jesus said that anyone who does not start by acknowledging this is not capable of hearing his amazing words about the loving graciousness of God: and why, at the heart of every act of worship, there are words of repentance and words of forgiveness.

If that were all that Christmas says it would be sufficient cause for joy. Yet there is more. For the meaning of the incarnation is only properly entered into when what happened once in history is seen to happen again and again and again as Christ is (as it were) born in us and takes control of our lives. For Christmas is not then. It is now.

'What does it avail me' asks St Augustine, 'that this birth of Christ is always happening if it does not happen in me?' And if, beyond the Christmas lights, beyond the carols and the crib and the presents and all the things that delight our eyes and our stomachs, we can from our hearts answer 'Yes' to God's love as that is known in Jesus Christ, then we shall indeed know the joy of Christmas. Then the Christ who came first at Bethlehem to call us home to God is reborn in us and takes possession of our hearts.

19

An Anchor for Our Lives

The hope set before us is like an anchor for our lives. Hebrews 6.19

I shall never forget that most telling and poignant image of one brave Chinese student in 1989 standing alone before the advancing tanks in Tiananmen Square and then darting and weaving before them in a vain attempt to block their inexorable path. It was at once an act both foolish and magnificent, futile and ennobling. He had signed his death warrant, and yet his action said in one unforgettable image that, sinful and weak as we often are, the human spirit may be crushed but will not in the end be defeated. His was an action that spoke louder than words.

There are other times when words are as powerful as actions, as in the resistance to tyranny which after many years at last triumphed in much of Eastern Europe. This freedom was not achieved overnight, but by steady and persistent pressure often in the form of words: the words of poets, playwrights, journalists. When words are used to express the values which make us human over against actions which devalue us and curtail our freedom they take wing and they endure. Vaclav Havel put it like this:

> In the beginning was the Word, and the Word was the source of all creation. And I believe in the power of words to change history. For I inhabit a system where words can prove mightier than ten military divisions, where Solzhenitsyn's words of truth were regarded as something so dangerous that it was necessary to deport him. Yes, in the part of the world I inhabit the word Solidarity was capable of shaking an entire power bloc.

No lyric, no poem, no unarmed student has ever stopped a tank. Yet words in the hands of a poet, words which arise from a source deep within our shared humanity, such words are able to celebrate a truth which is more powerful than any political system. They guarantee the survival, in the face of the oppression and darkness of martial law, of that which is just and noble and honourable: the survival of that which is divine in each of us because it is implanted by God. And we know that is true because of Christmas.

In the harsh and oppressive society of the Roman Empire it took a poet, St John, to put into words the significance of what God has done in Christ. 'In the beginning was the Word, and the Word was made flesh and dwelt among us, full of grace and truth.' 'Words', claims Havel, 'have the power to change history.' And here, uniquely here, the Word and the action are one. The Word of God and the life of the man Jesus. The Word made flesh. The most unpredictable event in history. And the most joyful.

St John tells of one who looked men and women in the eye, whoever they were – Jew, Samaritan, Greek, Roman, friend or foe, good or bad – and related to them as children of the God who was his Father and their Father. He drew a few of them to himself to embody his way of living so that under God it might become the way for all humankind.

And some 30 years later, when Jesus stands bound and condemned to die, crushed but not defeated, John the poet puts into Pilate's mouth the words, 'Behold the Man!' Look, here is Man. Here is the true human life. 'We saw for a moment', writes Virginia Woolf in her novel *The Waves*, 'laid out among us the body of the complete human being, whom we have failed to be but at the same time, cannot forget. All that we might have been (and might still be) we saw.'

Here in this Word made flesh. Here in this vulnerable man who has drawn them to himself and taught them the meaning and costliness of love, and who is now to teach them in the face of suffering the meaning of trust, and in the face of death the meaning of hope.

'The hope set before us is like an anchor for our lives.' The world may not be much less dangerous, and certainly is no less sinful from year to year. Yet acts of courage and the words which inspire such actions renew our hope in the resilience of the human spirit which takes its life from God, and renew our faith in the power of words to change the course of history. And Christmas affirms these truths and takes us to the heart of them. It goes behind them and beyond them. Christmas declares that the Word which changed history most profoundly, the Word that continues to illuminate our humanity, the Word that shows that every man, woman and child in the world is lovable and infinitely precious, is the Word made flesh. The Word that once took the form of a tiny, vulnerable child lying in the straw. He, and he alone, has the power to change our lives and make us whole and free. He and he alone, is the hope who is set before us that is like an anchor for our lives.

'I give you my Word', says God. So what do we reply? To celebrate Christmas, to know the joy of Christmas, is to say 'Amen'; to say 'Yes' in the deepest part of our being to that word God has spoken in Christ, and to look on Bethlehem as the place where God came to us in his Son and took us by the hand that he might bring us home.

20

The Awesome Truth of the Word Made Flesh

The Word was made flesh . . . full of grace and truth. John 1.14

Words, in the hands of a poet, can illuminate the familiar scene. And words, as used by all of us, give flesh to abstract thoughts – they are the language in which we make a declaration of love, share an insight, describe an experience or express a belief. And words are the only tools I have on Christmas Day with which to try and communicate once again the awesome truth of the Word made flesh: to take what is eternal and of God and relate it to our familiar lives.

I must therefore choose my words with the greatest care and speak from my own centre. For unless I give you something of myself, unless it is a kind of act of love, I shall only be communicating at the most trivial level. And you, for your part, if we are to share in this remarkable give-and-take of human communication, must give me something of yourself: your time and your attention.

What is true of our words, our means of communication, is true of the God in whose image we are made. And at Christmas we witness to the truth that the unimaginably mysterious source of all things to whom we give the name of God has chosen to reveal something of himself: to communicate with us on our terms. To say 'the Word is made flesh' is to say 'a child is born': a unique human being who speaks words which give flesh, which embody a whole new concept of God as Father. Here is love earthed in the particular words of the man Jesus.

But what if, for one reason or another, you cannot hear the words addressed to you? In Westminster Abbey we held a most unusual service to mark the centenary of the Royal Association for the Deaf. Almost everyone in the abbey that day was profoundly deaf, so that every word of the service had to be communicated not in words but in sign language by people placed in the quire and transepts. It was a revelation: a whole new kind of language – that of hands and of arms and body – with which to convey words and concepts. And while the gestures followed a general pattern there was a great variety of presentation that depended on the personality of the one doing the signing.

Near me a young woman interpreter signed with extraordinary grace and expressiveness, and into my mind with a quite new meaning came St John's words: 'The Word was made flesh . . . full of grace and truth.' And here was a reminder that for communication to be effective, words and actions must go hand in hand, and express the personality of the communicator. The Word is made flesh, 'God was in Christ' – God, in a particular man at a particular time – God, expressed through a particular personality, and revealed in a man whose words were perfectly mirrored and earthed in his actions.

Who can now say for certain which of the recorded words of Jesus actually came from his lips, but who can doubt those actions which are the seedbed of the Christian faith? What could better communicate the Christlike nature of God than a man who loves, and therefore gives his whole attention to each individual he meets – a man who enjoys eating good meals with bad people, who heals the sick, forgives the sinful and feeds the hungry? Here is a man who makes himself vulnerable even to the point of dying, a man who, when nailed to a cross, forgives his persecutors and loves his enemies. Here is a man who, on the far side of death, invited his doubting disciples to touch his hands and his wounded side. God's word is expressed in this man's living and dying and rising; in Jesus love is made flesh.

So Christmas is the turning point of history, nothing less than the earthing of the eternal God in his creation. In Jesus, God gives us his final and definitive word, so far as our lives here are concerned, about himself and about our destiny as his children. Despite the darkness, the pain and the evil all about us, despite the clamour, the greed and the blindness of the world, Christianity speaks – and will continue to speak – to those who said and to those who continue to say: I believe in God. I trust this Word made flesh at Christmas, this love become incarnate in Jesus Christ.

Words matter. They are the way we express ourselves and share our experiences and instincts and pains and joys. And with our words we can affirm or we can wound. Yet words are often ephemeral things: here one minute, gone the next, easily forgotten.

But not words which are given flesh; the deepest and truest definition of communication is God's definition. It is quite simply the giving of yourself in love, the giving of your attention to whoever is before you, so that you may affirm their value and (perhaps) meet their need. If that is so, then the one born at Christmas is the supreme communicator, in his words and in his actions, for they are of a piece and both show plainly the love of God.

God cannot communicate in a vacuum. He needed to be enfleshed in Mary's child. 'And what does this birth of Christ avail me', asked St Augustine, 'if it does not happen (now) in me?' So now it is our words tied to our actions that alone can communicate the truth and the forgiveness and the compassion of God as that is experienced in Jesus Christ. That is why Christmas Day is for all who claim to be Christians a day for wonder. A day, inevitably, for penitence. But, above all, a day when we celebrate and affirm our faith in the Christlike God who invites us to discover and serve him in one another and so sets us on the road to heaven.

21

A Wordless Yes

Truly I tell you, unless you change and become like children, you will never enter the kingdom of heaven. Matthew 18.3

John Taylor, for many years Bishop of Winchester, sent to his friends each year a Christmas poem. This one describes holding his grandchild in his arms before a bright candle on the Christmas tree.

Over the swinging parapet of my arm
your sentinel eyes lean gazing. Hugely alert
in the pale unfinished clay of your infant
face,
they drink light from this candle on the tree.
Drinking, not pondering, each bright thing you
see,
you make it yours without analysis
and, stopping down the aperture of thought
to a fine pinhole, you are filled with flame.

Give me for Christmas, then, your kind of
seeing,
not studying candles – angel, manger, star –
but staring as at a portrait, God's I guess,
that shocks and holds the eye, till all my
being,
gathered, intent and still, as now you are,
breathes out its wonder in a wordless yes.

'Give me for Christmas, then, your kind of seeing.' The way a child sees, with his or her whole attention: so absorbed in what lies before their eyes that they are lost in wonder.

We are, says Jesus, if we would know the Kingdom of God, to become like children. So may we at Christmas look beyond the little lights of angel, manger, star, shepherds, tree and gifts, and see in this child and the man he became, God: God with us in Jesus Christ, the light of the world. Never again need we doubt that at the heart of things there is a loving Creator and that we are loved.

Give me for Christmas, then, your kind of seeing,
not studying candles – angel, manger, star –
but staring as at a portrait, God's I guess,
that shocks and holds the eye, till all my being,
gathered, intent and still, as now you are,
breathes out its wonder in a wordless yes.

22

Is Your God Man Enough to Cry?

And the Word became flesh. John 1.14

I thank you, God, for this most amazing day!

Christmas Day is a day to astonish us and fill us with wonder, to cut through our chatter, to reduce us to silence and bring us to our knees. If it does not, then perhaps that is because we have tamed it, domesticated it, reduced it to what we can handle and feel at home with: carols and presents and mince pies. For the truth it contains is mind-blowing. As St John puts it: 'the Word became flesh.'

A child is born in the dark among the beasts – and nothing can ever be the same again. The all-holy and powerful Creator declares himself once and for ever to be with us and on our side, enfleshed, incarnate in our world which is also his world.

In late September 1991 I spent a week at Baylor University in Waco, Texas. It's the custom of the students there to use the pavements as a kind of university message service. They chalk on the sidewalk, 'Happy birthday, John', or 'Tennis match, Monday at 6.' Crossing the road one day on my way to give an address, I was faced with these astonishing words chalked in large letters on the kerb: 'Jesus wept. Is your God man enough to cry?' And I thought, that is spot-on for Christmas Day. Is your God man enough to cry?

Whoever wrote that understood. Understood what Christmas is about. Understood what Christians mean by the incarnation. Understood the significance of the title Emmanuel, which means God-with-us. Is your God man enough to cry? To be disclosed, once upon a time, in a crying baby – a fragile child whose skull is almost crushed by Herod's soldiers? To be revealed, once in history, in a vulnerable man weeping at the death of his beloved friend Lazarus? To be seen, once, in the words and actions of a man who is arrested, tortured and crucified? Is your God man enough to cry, to suffer and to die? Here is the Christian mystery, the ultimate paradox. Faced with a truth of such stunning import, our instinct is to tame it, to simplify it, to domesticate God by cutting him down to our size. But Christmas is not about the domesticating of God. It's about the humanizing of God: God revealed once in time wearing our shape. God who is never less than the all-powerful Creator of all that is, seen and unseen, yet who chooses to disclose the reality of his love in the only way we can begin to understand it: in the form of a child and the man that child became. The creative and all-powerful Word that was with God in the beginning is reduced to a child who must learn his first halting words at his mother's knee: a child who must himself first learn from Mary and Joseph the very meaning of love. Here is a mystery to amaze us and fill us with wonder, to reduce us to silence and bring us to our knees.

Being a Christian means seeing the face of God, just for a moment, just for a little while, and being changed by what you have seen. For if the all-holy God can reveal himself once in a stable then where may he not be found? If the all-holy God can be disclosed in the birth of a peasant's child, and the death of a carpenter on a gibbet, we can never be sure again where he may not appear or to what lengths he may not go in his gentle and loving pursuit of us.

We are right to look for him in our churches, and indeed the God we know in Christ is with us as we worship him, with us (as he promised) in the breaking of the bread, yet he also is to be found in places where we don't expect to find him and in unpredictable forms, so that we may reject him or fail to recognize him: disguised as the loved one to whom we no longer give our full attention, or as the hungry child we do not have to feed, or as that lonely neighbour we do not have to comfort, or that asylum-seeker, on whom we can turn our back. It is this truth of the hidden Christ that causes Mother Teresa to say, if you ask her why she cares for any human being in need, that she is 'serving Jesus under the distressing disguise of the poorest of the poor.'

The Russian writer Turgenev once dreamed that he was in a village church together with the peasant congregation. A man comes to stand beside him: 'I did not turn towards him, but immediately I felt that this man was Christ.' After a bit he turns towards him and perceives a face like everyone's face, 'a face like all men's faces . . . and the clothes on him like everyone else's.' Turgenev is astonished: 'What sort of a Christ is this? . . . such an ordinary, ordinary man.' He concludes: 'Suddenly I was afraid – and came to my senses. For I realized that it is just such a face – a face like all men's faces – that is the face of Christ.'

He too had learned the awesome and mysterious meaning of Christmas that is lurking there beneath the tinsel and the fairy lights, the discovery of the God who is with us and within us and on our side for ever – the Christlike God whom we may find in the places and the people where we least expect him: and the only God who is man enough to cry.

23

God's Self-Portrait

The Word was made flesh. John 1.14

If I say 'I give you my word', that may mean, 'You can trust me, I won't let you down.' Or it may mean, a bit more profoundly, 'I want to take some inner truth that is personal and important to me and share it with you in the only way I can. In words. I must take the 26 letters of the alphabet and mould and shape them in order to flesh out the truth as I see it.' The words must come from my heart and be consistent with my life if they're not to be banalities that cost me nothing. In other words: unless I give you in my words something of myself, unless it is, if you like, a small act of love, and unless you respond by giving me something of yourself – your attention – then there's no real communication, just a small disturbance of the air.

The story of Christmas is, of course, a love story: the story of how God communicates with us, of how he gives us his word, that is to say the perfect expression of himself, and translates it into the only language we can understand, human speech backed by a human life. That's what St John means when he says, 'The Word was made flesh.'

The analogy I want to pursue is not simply that of a wordsmith but also of an artist. For St Augustine's comment on those words of St John is this: 'The Word is, in a way, the *art* of the almighty and wise God.' The Word – Jesus Christ – is God's supreme work of art – if you like, his self-portrait.

Think of how an artist uses his materials – canvas, paint, stone, wood – to convey a truth through form and colour: how he gives flesh to his vision. Any work of art is a way of speaking. It is an attempt to find images that will tell us something true, something of lasting value, about a person or a landscape or an object. It starts with what is invisible – an idea, a thought, a way of seeing – which is then enfleshed in a painting or a sculpture that you can see and touch. Michelangelo sees in his mind's eye the complete perfection of a human figure within the rough block of stone, and chisels away until it emerges. The invisible is made visible before our eyes: the idea, the Word is made flesh.

The mark of a great artist (and this applies equally to a poet, novelist or composer) is that they see ordinary things in a unique and special way, and also have the power of choosing images that take us beyond the mere surface of things to an awareness of their value and meaning, their beauty or their terror. A painting may show us a human face, a tree, a birth or a death as we have never seen them before, and the greatest works of art can reduce us to a kind of silent wonder in the face of some aspect of beauty or truth about the human condition. That kind of truth is compelling just because it seems to impinge upon us from outside ourselves and yet speaks directly to our hearts.

I think of a visit I paid to the museums of Amsterdam. In the first I stood and gazed for a long time at Rembrandt's portrait of his son, Titus. What a painting! In it Rembrandt is making a profound statement about the unique value of this boy to his father, but also a universally true statement about human vulnerability and the transient nature of beauty that will be as true in 1,000 years as it was for him and is for us. Yet he is miraculously embodying his vision in a square of canvas and some dried paint: a word made flesh.

In the Van Gogh Museum there are paintings of cornfields and sunflowers and portraits of people in which van Gogh uses colour of such radiance as to suggest they have an eternal dimension, and round the heads of his portraits he creates such an effect of light as to suggest the divine potential in every human being.

If a human artist feels impelled to communicate what lies within him in this way, how much greater must be God's yearning to communicate something of himself to his creatures! The psalms and the book of Job are written by those who know the created world to be shot through with order, harmony and beauty, a miraculous and powerful work of art; but only in Jesus, only in this unique and particular birth, is the inmost nature of

God at last revealed to be not only power but love. What we cannot know for ourselves is now revealed to us – fleshed out – in a series of images that we can understand and to which we can respond: in a wordless, newborn child and in the man that child became. Those who tell his story present us with memorable images, as an impressionist painter or a poet would, images that point beyond themselves to the very heart of reality itself. They tell a story of a star and angels and shepherds and a stable – of blind men seeing, deaf men hearing, of the dead raised to new life. Of a shared meal, a kiss of betrayal, a fire in a courtyard, a nailing to a cross of wood and an empty garden tomb.

They say to us: 'This man whom we loved and followed we now know to be nothing less than God giving us, in a most costly act of love, the essence of himself: bone of our bone, flesh of our flesh – Christ, "the image of the invisible God".'

God's self-portrait turns out to be at once more ordinary and more extraordinary than anyone had dreamed. As ordinary as the man in the village carpenter's shop: as extraordinary as every human being is shown by this man to be when we turn and open ourselves in trust and gratitude to our Father's love.

All I have to offer you at Christmas are words. If I want you to know they are truly what I most deeply believe I can only add: 'I give you my word.' Which is, of course, what God says in Jesus. And in two senses: with a capital W and with a small one. In the first sense, Jesus Christ is the Word made flesh, the human face of God, the true expression of the inmost heart of God in the only language we can understand. 'Whoever has seen me has seen the Father.'

But if 'word' is put in lower case, then we may hear God saying in Christ:

Trust me. I give you my word that I am on your side. Even when things are at their darkest I am the God who is with you, in your joys, in your afflictions, and eventually in your dying. For I have been there before you in my Word that was once made flesh.

24

Seeing the World with Love

Come and see. John 1.39

I keep a very occasional diary. Glancing through its sparse entries as the year ends, I spot this:

> Tuesday 2 February. Attend a meeting with a group of people just back from Bosnia. They describe some of the unspeakable horrors being perpetrated on women and on prisoners, and show photographs. For me the horror is frozen into one single image: a dead child's charred hand emerging from the ruins of a house in a Muslim village after a Croatian vengeance attack. On my way home I slip into the National Gallery to counter such images of horror by standing first before Crivelli's breathtaking annunciation of the angel to Mary and then a self-portrait of Rembrandt. Later, at Evensong, it being the Feast of the Presentation, the choir sing the canticles to the lovely setting of Stanford in G.

Question: How do you hold these things together in your mind?

I want to try and answer my own unresolved question. Many would dismiss the ordered beauty of worship as an indulgent irrelevance amid the dark realities in which we live, when we are constantly made aware of the human potential for wickedness and the hellish nature of parts of our world. 'We *should* be aware of suffering, torture and injustice', writes the poet P. J. Kavanagh. 'There are however times when our preoccupation with these things would seem to imply that our forefathers lived in kindergartens and sucked their thumbs, whereas we alone have found the courage to open our eyes and look at the world.'

Past centuries – and certainly the world into which Jesus was born – were equally dark and cruel and violent. And yet what survives of them is not the horror but the astonishing ability of certain human beings to explore truth, to create and capture beauty, in wood and stone and clay, in words and paint and music, and to live lives of surpassing courage, dedication and compassion. It is true that no poem has ever stopped a tank, but there are poems, paintings, buildings, compositions, that have stopped people dead in their tracks, amazed and moved by the work of the human spirit, their understanding of what it means to be a person suddenly enlarged.

Why, when I wanted to match the distressing image of that Muslim child's charred hand did I go and stand in front of an annunciation and a Rembrandt? Is not the life of a single child worth more than a whole gallery of paintings? Yes, it is; but it is the gift of certain artists to open our eyes and enlarge our understanding of the mystery of what it means to be human. 'I try to create round the heads of my portraits', wrote van Gogh, 'such an effect of light as to suggest the divine potential in every human being.' And if such artists feel compelled to communicate what lies within them, then God's yearning to communicate something of himself to his creatures must be unimaginably greater, especially if it's true that his inmost nature is not revealed in the terrifying power of the whirlwind but in stillness, in acts of suffering and humble service, and in that giving of yourself to others that we call love. What we could never have suspected in a million years, what many still do not begin to understand, was once and for all time revealed – fleshed out – in a human life. In a wordless newborn child, and in the man that child became.

Those who tell his story present in it compelling images, as a painter might: images that point beyond themselves to the very heart of reality. They tell of the blind seeing, the deaf hearing, the outcast welcomed, the guilty set free. Of a shared meal, a traitor's kiss and a friend's denial. A nailing to a cross and an empty tomb. But above all, of men and women being set free to live in the spirit of the one who showed us how, against the odds, the world may begin to be changed by those who see it and its people with love. 'Come and see', says the artist, 'how even the most unlikely subject-matter is transformed when the light falls on it in a certain way.' 'Come and see', say the Gospels, 'what God looks like, and what people look like, in the light of Christ.'

Thus, what Christmas shows is doubly revealing: God in Christ revealing as much as we need to know about him for the present, but equally, God in Christ unmasking who we truly are, each of us in our human mystery – our understanding of what it means to be a person not simply enlarged, but transformed.

How do you hold these things together – the horror of the burned or murdered child and the wonder of a great work of art or of Stanford's setting for Mary's Magnificat? You do so by understanding that both speak the truth of the human condition, but the deeper and more powerful truth is the second. Once that wonder is lost, once the mystery of human life is denied, once we marginalize the holy and the transcendent, then human life does become cheap and expendable, and it becomes possible to kill or torture or treat with contempt other human beings with scarcely a second thought.

Christmas is not just about the birth of a child once. It is about a change as profound as that between blindness and sight. It is about the recovery of wonder. It is about being wise enough to fall silent in the face of mystery. It is about recognizing a Christlike God whose presence permeates his world. It is about trying and failing and trying and failing but never giving up trying to look upon the world and each other with love. It is about resisting all that would drag us down and diminish us because Christ has for ever opened our eyes to see who we truly are.

And, best of all, it is about continuing to journey in trust and hope, for that will mean that the Word who once took flesh in Bethlehem will have found the lodging he seeks in our own hearts.

25

A Permanent State of Mind

God has never been seen by anyone; but if we love one another, God
lives in us, and his love is perfected in us. 1 John 4.12

In my mind's eye I can see a particular clutch of churches, five
potent, numinous places that touch the heart.

One is a small pilgrim chapel on a high hill in Dorset erected
by Benedictine monks. It has stood like a beacon since the four-
teenth century, and lying below on all sides is a patchwork of
fields, the winding coast and the sea.

Memory number two is similar: a dark dry-stone oratory on
the Dingle Peninsula in southwest Ireland, one of the earliest
surviving places of Christian worship. It's an unadorned chapel
shaped like an upturned boat, a place where prayer has been
valid for 1,300 years, while outside are grazing sheep and the
dazzle of grass and sea in the June sun.

Memory number three is the great vaulted church of St Ambrose
in Milan, with a tenth-century pulpit. The skeleton of St Ambrose,
dressed in chasuble and mitre, somewhat startlingly, lies in a glass
case in the crypt, for it was in the basilica on this site that in the
fourth century he baptized St Augustine.

The fourth memory is that most numinous of Romanesque
churches, Vézélay, with its medieval capitals and its soaring
honey-coloured arches. I was there as they were preparing for
the evening Mass, the small community of monks and nuns
chanting timeless psalms.

But the final, abiding memory is the Monastery of Zagorsk,
north of Moscow, in October: for centuries a most holy place of
pilgrimage, as St Sergius, Russia's patron saint, is buried there.
As you kneel at his silver tomb, at which priests continually read
the Gospels and women chant the alleluias amid the soft glow of

candles and beneath the rich screen of icons, you remember how once its doors were closed by Stalin, its monks exiled or shot.

A hilltop pilgrim chapel, an early Irish Christian oratory, a north Italian shrine, a Romanesque basilica, and a Russian monastery. All of us could name a thousand more such places of worship by which we have been moved.

So they stand, these churches, stretching across the earth and across the centuries, silent witnesses in wood and stone. But witnessing to whom? To answer 'God' is not enough. For, as St John writes: 'God has never been seen by anyone', and it would be mere superstition to build shrines, as the Athenians did, 'to the unknown God', some remote and unimaginable Being.

But ... and it's the 'but' that saves us: the 'but' that is Christmas. For the truth is that God would not be God if he could be fully known to us, but God would not be God if he could not be known at all. And this unseen, unchanging God, so the Christmas gospel declares, is love, and the very essence of love is the readiness to give itself away. So St John writes: 'God has not been seen by anyone, but everyone who loves is the child of God and knows God, for God is love ... And God showed his love by sending his only Son into the world that we might have life through him.'

Every church in the world exists because of that divine 'but' – God acting in what we call the incarnation – for Christmas is the yearly celebration of the truth that crowns all other truths.

Here, in this extraordinary act of love, God makes his nature known in the only language we can speak or understand – human language. One child is born, and grows to be the man who alone of all our race looks at the ineffable mystery we call God and claims that his name is 'Father.'

Here is mystery and wonder too, and we who seek to speak of this life-changing truth find that words buckle and bend under its weight. As the poet Edwin Muir said: 'The Word that was once made flesh we have made words again.'

Whole libraries are filled with attempts to explain this mystery, the belief that Jesus Christ 'is the image of the invisible God', and that self-giving, suffering Love lies at the heart of creation. And at one level all such attempts are bound to fail. Yet all I can tell you is that I know nothing else that comes near to making sense of life, nothing else that begins to answer some of the deep and puzzling questions we all ask in times of darkness.

I can understand those who cannot believe the Christian claim. For it is an all-but-incredible claim. What I find much harder to understand is that those who do believe can do so without any sense of astonished wonder. For here is a mystery that ought to bring us to our knees. Here is a truth that has inspired the greatest music and art, and changed the civilized world. Yet too often we have tamed it, and reduced it to what we can handle and feel at home with: the familiar carols, the homely crib, and presents and mince pies once a year. All of which are fine, but not as a substitute for wonder. Which is why, although Christmas is not so much a single day as a permanent state of mind, we still need the challenge of Christmas Day itself to remind us that without it, there could only be shrines dedicated 'to the unknown God.'

Instead, Christian churches famous or not stand like silent witnesses – churches built by those who have looked at the mystery of the Word made flesh and believed it. Tiny pilgrim chapels, early Christian oratories, Romanesque churches, the Orthodox monasteries of Russia, the white, clapboard chapels of New England – each continues to speak in its own tongue of the all-holy God who reveals himself once and for ever to be with us, incarnate in our world which is also his world, enfleshed in the one born in a stable who was full of grace and truth.

26

The Silence of Gratitude and Wonder

*The Word was made flesh and lived among us . . . full of grace
and truth. John 1.14*

I have a problem with second-hand bookshops – well, any
sort of bookshop really. I can't walk past them: the tug is too
great. In the basement of one I know well it says, 'Second-
hand Theology', and I think, 'Yes, most of it is.' Second-hand.
Like most sermons: second-hand, even third- or fourth-hand.
People's ideas about other people's ideas about God. Endless
words about 'the Word.'

So I tend to make for the poetry section across the way. For
poets know that words must come new-minted and from the
heart, and they employ telling images and metaphors, just as
the Christmas stories do, to point to the heart of the mystery.
The mystery, above all, of one particular birth that changed the
whole course of human history.

But it takes a first-hand theologian, St John, to bring to the
simple charm and wonder of the story of that birth the insight
of a poet. Not simply 'Once upon a time there was a baby', but
'The Word was made flesh and dwelt among us, full of grace and
truth.' Here is the truth and it is full of wonder: the secret of the
universe is revealed within the human cry of a newborn child.
Here is nothing less than the earthing of God in his creation.
And without that insight into the mystery that we call the incarnation, Christmas can dissolve into no more than a sentimental,
antiquated tale.

Yet this, in every sense, was the moment when *before* turns
into *after*. Everything now must be redefined. Everything: start-
ing with God. Out goes the fear of an unknown God. In its place
we discover a God who in Jesus is saying: 'But I am not like that.

I am like this!' When Jesus says 'He who has seen me' – that is to say, my compassion, my vulnerability, my desire to serve, my concern for the undesirables – 'he who has seen me has seen the Father', he isn't making a claim about himself. He isn't saying: 'I am Godlike.' He is declaring the truth about God. He is saying: 'God, who is your Father, is Christlike.'

But if Christmas redefines God, it also redefines our hopes and our dreams. I can remember going to Southwark Cathedral for the World AIDS Day service. Some there were mortally ill, yet it was all about their hopes and their dreams. For there, suspended above the chancel and caught in the beams of two spotlights, was what Native American Indians call a dreamcatcher. A large vertical wooden hoop hung there, and woven into its frame was a patterned cobweb of strings all meeting in the centre, full of knots and spaces, and beneath the hoop hung feathers and tassels. A dreamcatcher catches your hopes and your dreams. The bad ones, the destructive ones, are caught in the knots and the sun's rays evaporate them. The good ones find their way through the holes to the feathers and lie there safely stored, ready and waiting for when you may need to use them.

I like the thought of God as dreamcatcher – our destructive acts and desires caught in the knots of his love and evaporating in the rays of his forgiveness – our good hopes, our dreams of peace and justice, our acts of kindness and compassion, stored up for future use. For we live in a world which is full of bad dreams and very short of hope, given to cynicism and sometimes despair. For what is more natural in the face of repeated breakdowns of civilized life and behaviour – nations ravaged by war, violence and disease, people defeated by poverty and unemployment, others by the hurts life brings – than to become cynical or despairing? Yet hope as Christians understand it is not blindness to the darkness of human life. It isn't an absurdly cheerful optimism, the conviction that something will turn out well in the end. It goes much deeper than that. It is the certainty that life makes sense, however it turns out, and that there is nothing that cannot be redeemed and something of good brought out of it.

I once heard a Jewish rabbi, imprisoned as a child in a Nazi concentration camp, say: 'Jews have an incurable hope.' So have Christians. For hope is a state of mind, not a state of the world. It is a dimension of the soul, an orientation of the heart, and it is anchored beyond our everyday horizons in the God revealed in Jesus Christ. It is anchored too in what Jesus revealed about the dignity and value of every human being in God's sight: not just God redefined in the light of Christmas, but every one of us redefined as well.

Second-hand theology turns these Christmas truths into a wordy address. Yet God didn't offer those first farm workers and fishermen second-hand theology. He offered them at first hand the Word made flesh, full of grace and truth. He still does. And he invited a response. And he still does that too. In the beginning was the Word, but in the end is silence. The silence when all our halting words come to an end. It is the silence of gratitude – and wonder.

PART 3

Epiphany

27

Christic is Made the Sure Foundation
Week of Prayer for Christian Unity

God has made known his hidden purpose, namely that the universe,
all in heaven and all on earth, might be brought into a unity in Christ.
Ephesians 1.9–10

Once when I was a parish priest I decided to mark the Week of
Prayer for Christian Unity by giving a rose bush to all the city
centre churches of the other major traditions. Choosing the roses
was quite an exercise in tact. I mean, how about Iceberg for the
somewhat unyielding Baptists? And how would the Methodists
take to Whisky Mac? In the end I played safe and gave them all
Peace; and it is in the spirit of the peace and love of Christ that I
offer these thoughts.

On 10 May 1941, in a terrible raid, the Houses of Parliament
and Westminster Abbey were bombed. The abbey was saved by
the courage of the firefighters, but much was destroyed and the
Deanery was gutted by fire. The very next day, at one of the low-
est points in the war, there was a meeting at the Stoll Theatre,
Kingsway, of the Sword of the Spirit, a Catholic-sponsored
group concerned with Christian unity. On the platform were
Cardinal Hinsley and the Anglican Bishop of Chichester, George
Bell, together with the Moderator of the Free Church Federal
Council. Cardinal Hinsley closed the meeting with these words:

Our unity must not be in sentiment and in word only; it must
be carried into practical measures. Let us have a regular system of consultation and collaboration . . . to agree on a plan of
action which will win the peace when the din of battle is over.

At this point Bishop Bell whispered to the cardinal, 'Eminence, may we say the Our Father?' and Hinsley at once led the whole assembly in the Lord's Prayer. It was such a surprising and unusual thing to do that it is recorded by Church historians, who also record that Hinsley was reproved by his fellow bishops for praying with heretics – though not, interestingly, by Rome.

Some 50 years on, despite all that still divides us, the scene is almost totally transformed. I think of the areas of ecumenical experiment that have sprung up all over the country – of Roman Catholics and Anglicans sharing churches, with joint baptism and confirmation services – of local Councils of Churches and joint study programmes. I think of the new Instrument for Unity, Churches Together in England, with the Roman Catholic Church now a full member. I think of Liverpool, previously a centre of particular bitterness, and of the working together of the Roman Catholic archbishop and the Anglican diocesan bishop. I think of the great service held in recent years when thousands packed Westminster Cathedral to mark the Second Vatican Council's Decree on Ecumenism, led by the Cardinal Archbishop, the Archbishop of Canterbury and the Free Church Moderator, when we sang 'Christ is made the sure foundation' to the tune Westminster Abbey. And in terms of the abbey, I think of a Catholic parish priest coming to baptize; of shared Catholic/Anglican weddings; of Catholic parish priests bringing their people for Mass at St Edward's shrine.

What recent years have seen is a quite new understanding of our deep and fundamental unity in Christ: 'Christ is made the sure foundation.' You cannot compare where we were when Bell hesitantly asked Hinsley if they might share in saying the Lord's Prayer, and where we are today, without being deeply aware of the gently probing and transforming action of God the Holy Spirit.

The chief work of the Spirit, said Jesus, will be to lead you into all truth. The search for the unity which Christ desires for his Church is, and must always be, seeking the truth about God, and the truth about God is Christ. Here is the truth that lies at the centre of our Christian life: God was in Christ, and now we are in Christ, and Christ in us.

'There is one body, one Spirit, one Lord, one faith, one baptism, and one God and Father of all.' The living truth that commands us, and demands a personal response is the Christmas truth of the incarnation, the truth that the Word became flesh, that God is revealed in the only terms we can understand, human terms: a God who is with us, speaking our language, suffering beside us and dying for us. This is the great uniting, central mystery, the truth that we need to understand more and more deeply throughout our lives. We, who have been divided by history, long for a visibly united Church, each tradition reunited with the other but not absorbed, still retaining its God-given diversity. But that lies in the still unimaginable future. What we can here and now recognize is our present, real and actual unity in Christ.

So we witness to and celebrate our unity in Christ. We celebrate our belief in the Christlike God, his mercy and his grace – in the reality of forgiveness, both divine and human – and our belief in our common life of prayer and sacrament. To believe in the unity Christ prayed for is to believe that all that is true, all that is of Christ in our present fragmented traditions, will one day be brought into one great united communion of the Holy Catholic Church.

But even that is not to go far enough. For that is not St Paul's vision. His vision is of the unity of the whole of humankind: 'God has now made known his hidden purpose,' he writes to the Ephesians, 'namely that the universe, all in heaven and all on earth, might be brought into a unity in Christ.' That is to say: there are no 'outsiders', for God's lively and inviting love is without bounds. And the Church exists to be a foretaste, to nurture and to anticipate the future of all our humanness.

Any unity we seek must be to that end: the kind of unity which allows those outside to get a whiff of their own true humanity, to glimpse with delight and hope the possibility of their own wholeness and reconciliation. As someone has said: 'The Church is the world-ahead-of-itself in which all things are related and if any part is missing then the whole is incomplete.'

It is that sense of incompleteness that makes us as individuals yearn for God. It is that sense of incompleteness that makes divided Christians long to be able to share at the same altar the body and blood of Christ, and sets before us a vision that, once it has seized you, will not let you go.

28

The Christian Journey
Week of Prayer for Christian Unity

Lord, to whom else can we go? You have the words of life. John 6.68

Isn't it strange that clergy are thought of as people who are easily shocked? For if you are a priest or any kind of counsellor you very soon discover there is nothing people can tell you about themselves that can ever really surprise you, not their anger or their jealousy or their fears, nor their loneliness or lack of confidence or their guilt: for you too are human. You too – in your moments of honesty – know these things in your own heart. But, being human, you too share that restless searching for God, that longing for beauty and fulfilment in a world where so much is mean and ugly and what is good and true is so elusive.

It was at once the most disturbing and the most healing aspect of coming face to face with Jesus of Nazareth that he saw into the heart. So when he chose, apparently so abruptly, Simon and Andrew and James and John as his first disciples, he was under no illusion about them. In St John's words, 'he knew what was in man.' He knew how fragile and feeble we are – how sinful and fallible; but he had this kind of double vision, so that he also saw what we have in us to become because we are made in God's likeness. He saw – none more clearly – the actual and the potential: both what we are and what we might be.

So he called ordinary, sinful folk to be with him, and his task was slowly and painfully and patiently to draw out of them a potential for loyalty and self-giving love they never knew they possessed. 'You *are* Simon the Fisherman; you *shall be* Peter the Rock.' 'You *are* Saul, scourge of the young struggling Church; *you shall* be Paul, its greatest teacher.'

'You are – you shall be.' The Christian life is not just a journey from birth to death. It is also a journey inwards, a discovery of your true self and the true nature of other people and the true nature of God. The Christian life, in St Augustine's phrase, is about 'becoming what you are.' Becoming more truly yourself as the loved child of God.

Yet following Christ, 'growing up into Christ', as St Paul calls it, doesn't mean losing your identity or becoming so unattractively pious as to be unrecognizable to your friends. It means the flowering of your personality because you have turned to face in a new direction. In all kinds of ways Peter is still recognizably Simon, and in all kinds of ways Paul is still recognizably Saul, but that energy and aggressive singlemindedness that made the latter so powerful a persecutor of the Church has been turned and channelled and used to different ends. Something – in fact, someone – has intervened to change their outlook at such a deep level that later they could only describe themselves as reborn. That experience, the experience of being confronted by Jesus Christ, the experience of knowing at the deepest level what it means to be loved, to be forgiven, to be believed in – that experience, then as now, changes everything. The experience it most resembles is falling in love. It is the story both of what you are and what you might be. It is called 'conversion.'

Don't be alarmed by that word. I know it sometimes sends out embarrassing vibes. For we are who we are and we shall respond to Jesus Christ in our own fashion. Some of us are emotional and extrovert creatures, while others are shy and gentle and withdrawn. Some are highly intelligent and some are bears of very little brain. Some have been so hurt by life that they are wounded and vulnerable. All our journeys and needs are different. And the God who calls us to respond to him in Jesus is the one who sees into the heart and knows we can only respond in our own fashion. We each have our own journey – but whether we actually choose to make the Christian journey will depend on the recognition that God does indeed meet us in Christ and invites our response.

For people like Saul that recognition comes with all the force of a lightning flash and they're never quite the same again. For others – perhaps for most of us – it is more like a slowly dawning realization that I am held in a relationship with one who is the very source of my being – that I am addressed by him by name and invited to respond to the one who in Jesus Christ is seen to be self-giving love.

When Simon and Andrew and James and John had upped and left their fishing boats to follow Jesus, and when they had got to know him and seen many who were attracted to him initially turn back shocked by his claims, Jesus said to them: 'How about you? Do you also want to leave me?'

And Simon the Fisherman who was to be renamed Peter the Rock replied: 'Lord, to whom else can we go? You have the words of life.'

29

From One Way of Seeing to Another
Week of Prayer for Christian Unity

I am the bread of life. Whoever comes to me will never be hungry, and whoever believes in me will never be thirsty. John 6.35

There is a story of a priest walking home in Liverpool one winter evening in the early 1930s when there was a severe depression and much poverty, and passing a crowded fish and chip shop. The owner of the shop was scooping up the chips and emptying them onto greaseproof bags. The priest had seen it a hundred times, but suddenly the whole scene took on a deeper significance. When he got home he wrote in his diary: 'All of a sudden, tonight, I saw the *glory* . . . the ordinary became the extraordinary. And in that context the proprietor became a symbol of the heavenly Father giving his children their daily bread.'

'All of a sudden I saw the glory.'

Now what some call 'miracles' St John calls 'signs' – and I find that a more helpful word. For signs point to a reality beyond themselves – but you have to have eyes to see and understand.

What St John does in his Gospel is to select some event and describe it at two levels. He tells a story of people at a wedding reception where the wine has run out, or a woman coming to draw water from a well, or a crowd hungry for food and far from home. In each case they meet Jesus, he does something for them, and for John these encounters are signs that point beyond themselves to eternal truths about God and how we encounter him. Here are stories of what men and women are doing in their ordinary lives – having a party, fetching water, gathering to hear a rabbi speak – but they are also stories of what God is doing at the level of Spirit and how he may be encountered in Jesus.

St John's concern in his Gospel is to open our eyes to two quite different ways of living and interpreting our lives. The first way is obvious: we eat and drink. We make a few friends and perhaps a few enemies. We marry and have children. We work and compete. We worry about money. Perhaps we fall sick. And eventually, we die. But there is a second and quite different way of understanding the world and your place within it, and that is in the light of Christ – for what Christ does is to impose on these same lives a quite new order of understanding. This new order speaks of change – indeed, transformation and new life – where the ruling principle is not the spirit of competition but the Spirit of love, and the pattern of society is one of compassion – people giving to each other what they really are, and accepting what others are, recognizing their differences, and sharing their vulnerability. To get from one way of seeing to the other – if, in short, we are to see something of the glory – we need what Jesus calls a new birth in which with new eyes and with God's grace we begin to encounter God in the world about us and in one another.

So when St John writes of the woman at the well he is choosing the *sign* of Jesus as the living water who constantly has the power to renew and refresh us. And in the sign of Jesus changing water into wine he is writing of the transforming power of God's love and the effect it can have on lives. And when he writes of Jesus taking bread and breaking it and satisfying the hunger of a huge crowd he is telling us that Jesus is the bread of life who satisfies our hunger at every level, and renews us at every Eucharist because he brings us the certainty of the Father's healing and forgiving love.

Thus, the 'signs of glory' around which St John weaves his Gospel all point to the glory of God's love as that is revealed in Jesus Christ. But those 'signs of glory' also point to the reality of his Spirit in our midst. For what John is telling us loud and clear is that ever since that day when Mary Magdalene discovered at dawn the empty tomb, and on the evening of which the disciples assembled to receive their commission, we have lived in the age of the Holy Spirit. And ever since the God we know in Jesus has spoken direct to human hearts and minds through his presence in our midst.

During the Week of Prayer for Christian Unity we are reminded that our history has divided us. Please God the Spirit is drawing us into a united Church which will be generous and diverse enough in its worship and interpretation of doctrine to contain us all in our infinite variety. We shall hasten the coming of that united Church if we recognize and celebrate the signs of glory which speak of that new order to which by our baptism and our sharing in the Eucharist we already belong.

'I am the living water.' 'I am the new wine.' 'I am the bread of life.' 'Those who come to me, and see in me my Father, and trust themselves to the transforming power of the Spirit, will never hunger or thirst.'

It's true our unity is incomplete, and we need to pray and grow together in many ways. Yet what unites Christians already is infinitely greater than anything that can divide us. It is our faith that God is made known in Jesus, and the knowledge that we are redeemed and forgiven, baptized and raised to new life, indwelt by the *one* Spirit, and members of the *one* indivisible body of Christ.

30

A Single Ray of Light
Week of Prayer for Christian Unity

The light shines in the darkness, and the darkness did not overcome it.
John 1.5

Sometimes the light from the winter sun strikes the great glass chandeliers in Westminster Abbey, and their prisms refract the light into all the colours of the rainbow: red and yellow and orange and green and blue and indigo and violet.

Beneath those chandeliers in the nave lies the body of Sir Isaac Newton, who first discovered by experimenting with just such a prism the behaviour of light. He placed his glass prism in the path of a candle in his rooms at Trinity College, Cambridge, and the spectrum was revealed. Each ray of light was refracted into its seven different colours, because the particular wavelength of each band makes it subject to a different degree of bending as it passes through the glass.

Picture, then, a single ray of light shining onto a prism, from which fan out the seven different colours of the rainbow. I ask you to lodge that picture in your mind.

Turn next to the story from St John's Gospel of 5,000 hungry people fed with five loaves and two fish. Some would call it a miracle. St John uses a different word and calls it a *sign*. And in his Gospel he has seven of them.

The purpose of a sign is to point to something beyond itself, some deeper truth that lies beneath the surface meaning, and John's signs are about extraordinary things happening to ordinary people when they encounter Jesus. The first concerns people at a wedding where the drink runs out and water is changed into wine. The second tells of a sick boy being healed. The third of a lame man finding he can walk again. The fourth of a hungry crowd being fed. The fifth of a blind man receiving his sight. The sixth of a dead man, Lazarus, being raised to life. And the seventh? Well, the seventh sign describes how this man, this healer and teacher, this worker of signs for others, is himself rejected, taken out and crucified in a barren place outside the city wall.

So what do these signs mean? At one level they are about people encountering Jesus. But at another level, for those with eyes to see, they are what the Prayer Book calls 'Signs of Glory.' For they point to a unique encounter with God. They say: 'This man was divine.' 'This man was revealing the Father in a unique way.' So from the story of the feeding of the 5,000 we see: 'This man is the living bread; he satisfies our hunger for God at the deepest level of spirit because he brings with him the certainty of the Father's healing and forgiving love.'

These seven signs are like a rainbow forming a single ray of light which shows us the light of the world, the one light that shines in the darkness and which, says St John, can never be quenched. They point to the truth of God's great decisive action in redeeming the world, and establishing a new creation in which those blind to the truth see, those deaf to it hear, the sinful find forgiveness, and even the dead are raised to new life. The final sign of glory is the sign God gives of his power to create and recreate when, at Easter, he raises Jesus from the dead.

Thus, there are two pictures. The first is the glass prism revealing first one, then another, colour of the rainbow, but all stemming from a single ray of light. The second picture is of St John composing his Gospel in old age, selecting with infinite care those signs that will show different aspects of Jesus' ministry and which together show him as the Light of the World, and point us to the truth that this man was God incarnate.

The Week of Prayer for Christian Unity reminds us of the divided state of the Church of God. We Christians are as diverse and varied as the colours of the rainbow, well aware that red is not orange, nor blue green. Though at one level we are divided and have been divided by history into our separate traditions, yet there is a deeper truth, for those with eyes to see the sign of the prism. Which is this: that each colour, each tradition, stems from a single ray of light, and the common source of our life is

Christ. All who believe that in Jesus we see God and put their faith in him are at the deepest level already *one* in Christ. We are those who have seen the signs of glory in the man Jesus – the sign of sinners forgiven, the sign of the hungry fed, blind eyes opened and deaf ears unstopped – the sign of the cross and the empty tomb.

We are *in* Christ – he is *in* us – and we look to him in all our splendidly rainbow-hued diversity as, in the darkness, the one true source of light.

31

A Controlled and Costly Anger

And Jesus made a whip of cords and drove the dealers in cattle and sheep and pigeons and the money-changers out of the temple, and upset their coins. John 2.15

There was once a king of whom it was said that, when he was angry, one of his eyes became so terrible that no one could bear to behold him, and the wretch upon whom it was fixed instantly swooned, and sometimes expired. For fear, however, of depopulating his kingdom, he wasn't angry all that often.

Anger is present in all of us. It is something we are born with, as natural as brown hair or blue eyes, and there's nothing more spectacularly angry than a frustrated baby. In some today anger is very near the surface, and the least incident – a traffic jam, say, or a careless word – will cause it to erupt. A lot of our anger needs to be recognized for what it is: cheap, easy-to-come-by anger – anger that is self-indulgent, a failure to get our own way, a letting-off of steam that is destructive – the child in us throwing our toys around.

However, there is a quite different kind of anger. 'And Jesus made a whip of cords and drove the dealers in cattle and sheep and pigeons and the money-changers out of the temple, and upset their coins.' That sort of anger is a controlled and costly anger – anger at injustice, anger at the exploitation of the poor by the traders and money-changers, for that's what the system meant. So not only were these merchants and money-changers abusing the house of God, but they were misusing their fellow men and women. That kind of anger is the very opposite of self-indulgence: it may even be our saving grace. Indeed, you could even call it Godlike; this righteous, controlled anger, for you cannot read the Bible and doubt the anger of God. The prophets and the psalms are full of it. Yet it is always more than matched by his compassion: 'The LORD is full of compassion and mercy, long-suffering and of great goodness; neither keepeth he his anger for ever.' For it's no expression of temper, this anger of God's – it is instead anger against injustice, an anger born of compassion and sorrow that we his children are so disobedient, so blind and deaf, so ready to exploit others, so constantly falling short of what we are created to be.

'And Jesus (in anger) made a whip of cords.' And when the Jews protested and questioned him he prophesied the destruction of the Temple itself and spoke of that different kind of temple, the temple of his own body in which the spirit of God dwells. Paul takes that concept a stage further: 'Do you not know that you are God's temple, and that God's Spirit dwells in you?' Christians have broadened this even further, claiming that all human beings are created in God's likeness, temples of his Spirit, and therefore sacred.

If that is so, should not certain facts be a cause in us of an anger that is born of compassion and a desire for justice? For instance: if you think of our world as a global village of 1,000 people, just 60 have control of the total income, while 700 are illiterate, of whom 600 live in shanty towns and 500 are hungry. Also, the proportion of money that nations spend annually on health care amounts to just three hours of what they spend each year on arms.

Should it not be a cause for anger that our society is so marred by greed, that in our country in recent years the rich have grown richer and the poor poorer? Think of the realities of unemployment, homelessness, racism. Children are exposed to drugs and corrupting images, and all of us are exposed to displays of crude violence, often sexual violence, that can blunt our sensitivity and poison our minds, and much of the tabloid press, in order to boost sales, is quite shameless in its invasion of privacy and its exploitation of people.

These are complex social, political and economic matters, and I am not making political points – nor, heaven forbid, am I aligning myself with what is known as the Moral Majority. Nothing is easier than indulging in generalizations, or the huffing and puffing of moral outrage at slipping standards and shifting values; and it's wrong to neglect so much that is good and constructive.

The point I am making is that, if we are concerned with building the Kingdom of God, then we *should* be angry at all forms of injustice, and all kinds of exploiting and spoiling of human beings made in God's likeness. But we should express our anger not by an irritable moralizing that costs us nothing. The controlled, righteous anger of Jesus cost him his life, for his kind of vision of a new order based on justice and human worth will always be subversive because it threatens the world's values and priorities. So if we believe that human beings are sacred, and that there are certain unchanging values that have their roots in the Kingdom, then each of us must ask ourselves how best we can protest against those worldly standards that work against a community based on justice, mercy, equity, truth and love. A bit more costly anger from the body of Christ would not come amiss.

32

The Power and the Wisdom of God

We are fools for the sake of Christ. 1 Corinthians 4.10

Westminster Abbey is an amazing place. I love it in the early morning or in the evening when the visitors have gone. You feel dwarfed by the graceful Gothic arches and fan vaulting high above your head. You are surrounded by the tombs of most of the kings and queens of England: by the shrine of St Edward the Confessor, and the graves and memorials of statesmen and scientists, poets and musicians. And how it's used! There are four services each day Monday to Saturday and five on Sunday. Once a week on an average there are large special services for different groups and organizations: for a hospital or a charity, for nurses or the police or a new Lord Mayor, for a famous statesman or actor who has died, on Remembrance Sunday or Battle of Britain Sunday or Commonwealth Day or Human Rights Day or World AIDS Day. At them all the choir sings superbly, and people of all nations, traditions and creeds come to the abbey in their thousands and tens of thousands. As they do on a Sunday morning in their hundreds and for what is central to our life: the Eucharist, with which each day begins and on which every Sunday is centred.

Yet sometimes, especially when I find myself processing round the abbey wearing a cope, I think to myself: watch it! For I know how deceptive and dangerous it can be to serve in such a privileged place. It is easy, in such a public and exposed position, to slip into the world's way of thinking.

It's then I remember with gratitude my years in South London, and later working in a huge council estate. I came to understand what it could mean to be part of a tiny minority (often less than 1 per cent of the population) meeting in the local church to worship God Sunday by Sunday and thought by many to be very foolish indeed.

St Paul talks in a number of places of 'the wise' and 'the foolish.' He means those who are 'wise' according to the world's standards, and he calls himself and his fellow-Christians 'foolish', 'fools for Christ's sake', for what could be more foolish than believing in a man who was crucified?

And I have to tell you that in the end what Westminster Abbey is about and what every other church is about is identical – and it is no doubt very foolish in the eyes of the world. For we all are those who believe that at the very heart of our faith is a unique, for some a foolish, story. It's a story that begins 'Once upon a time there was a child born in poverty among the beasts', and it ends 'Because of that child and the man he became and what he showed us of God, the world can never be the same place again.'

It's a story of a man who taught and healed and forgave people, who made no distinction and valued each one equally, and who suffered and was killed. Yet the story ends not with a cross but in the Easter garden. It is of course a love story whose meaning lies in one of the names given to the child: Emmanuel, for that means God-is-with-us. God is on our side. God loves us enough to have become one with us. When you look at the world and its unfairness and unpredictability, then what could be more foolish? Yet countless men and women have not only lived but died for that truth.

This man, whom we call Lord and Christ, takes what the world calls wisdom and turns it on its head. Those who follow him, he says, are to find their lives by losing them, by dying to themselves and living for others. They are to care more about serving than being served. They are to care more about forgiving their enemies than taking revenge on them, more about sharing what they have than making money, and more about creating a caring community than about the obsession with self-interest that is such an unattractive feature of our present political life.

Some who have followed Jesus worship in glorious cathedrals and abbeys, others churches or tiny mission halls. But what matters isn't the size of the building or its congregation. What matters is the desire of those who follow Jesus, often very foolishly and against all odds, to help build a caring, outgoing community, and to offer hope in the poverty and bleakness of many people's lives.

Often that seems an uphill battle, yet by the grace of God we persist, for we have a story to tell of a man nailed to a cross, yet one who now lives in all who believe in him. To many it is a foolish story, but to those who believe, it is nothing less than the power and the wisdom of God.

33

The Reality of God's Unswerving Love

Has no one condemned you? Neither do I condemn you. Go, and do
not sin again. John 8.10–11

In John 8.1–11 we see the quality that drew people to Jesus – and
has drawn them ever since. It's a breathtaking mixture of authority and truth and the most tender compassion. The setting is the
Temple in Jerusalem: the place where Judaism was to be found at
its purest, and Jesus is the one who is to transcend it and reveal
a new and different way. The charge is adultery. The woman's
guilt is not in doubt: she has been caught in the very act. The
inevitable sentence, as laid down in the Law of Moses? Stoning
to death. They bring her to Jesus not for him to act as judge, for
no rabbi had that authority, but for his opinion. A trap is set for
him: what will he do?

He doesn't condemn nor does he condone. He simply invites
this woman to see in him the love of God for what it is. In so
doing she is to be changed and set free by that small miracle we
call forgiveness.

Look at the scene again. It's the priests, the religious leaders,
who are using this woman in order to test Jesus: will he be seen
to disregard the Law of Moses? They suspect he is a blasphemer
and a law-breaker but they want proof. Here is spelled out in
miniature a conflict with which we still have to grapple: the conflict between the law and the gospel, justice and mercy.

The law, the Law of Moses, which Jesus is bound to observe as
a rabbi, demands she must be stoned. The good news he has come
to bring is that she may be forgiven. Jesus accepts there is a need
for law, for without it there would be moral and social anarchy,
but he rejects the whole system which the Pharisees represent,
whereby you earn or lose merit in the sight of God by living

your life according to a set of inflexible rules and principles, for that makes nonsense of the whole concept of God's freely given grace. It is this grace which is the heart of Jesus' teaching which to many has always been puzzling, if not shocking: this fact of God's uncalculating and indiscriminate love. Jesus sets it out time and again in parables like that of the labourers in the vineyard, where the last to be hired are treated every bit as generously as the first, because God's grace is like that – or the parable of the prodigal son, where the returning prodigal is welcomed without question with open arms to the jealous fury of his elder brother who has stayed at home.

There are no rules, then, which if we observe we will stand right with God. It isn't like that with God. There is only his generosity, and our response. There are no conditions, only his love. All are sinners: all may be forgiven. 'Let him who is without sin – the one who is completely innocent – throw the first stone', says Jesus. Those who have dragged this woman before him know they too stand convicted, and they go out one by one, 'the eldest first' you note, for even in defeat the Pharisees keep the correct order of precedence – rather like processions in the Church of England. Jesus says, revealing in this moment the eternal nature of the God he has come to make known: 'Has no one condemned you? Neither do I condemn you. Go, and do not sin again.'

It's a simple story, yet at the heart of it there lies a life-changing truth. For Jesus isn't saying to the woman: 'Your adultery doesn't matter.' Of course it matters. Anything which is an offence against love, anything which hurts and damages other people, matters. But neither does he play on her guilt or fear. He simply assures her that, whatever she has done and for whatever reason, she is not thereby cut off from the love of God. The moment we want God, we have him; the moment we turn to him recognizing our sinfulness and our need, we are met by his love and restoration.

This is what the Christian gospel is about. The powerful gospel, that is – not the feeble gospel. The feeble gospel sees Jesus as no more than an example for us to follow, and is concerned only about keeping the rules. The feeble gospel says: 'If you're sorry enough you may be forgiven.' The powerful gospel stems from the cross, from the one who loved so much that he gave his life for us. The powerful gospel says: 'You are redeemed! You are forgiven: turn and receive your forgiveness.' 'What shall I give up for Lent?' someone once asked me. 'Give up feeling guilty', I suggested, 'and learn to accept that you are forgiven.'

Being a Christian, therefore, isn't about keeping some set of rules, or about denying our real feelings or pretending to be other than what we are. It's about responding to the God who is love, responding to certain haunting images which show him to be so – a child in a stable – a man healing the sick and consoling the lost and the unloved – a man facing a woman caught in the very act of adultery and saying, 'Go, and sin no more' – a man washing his disciples' feet, breaking bread with them, dying for them on a cross, and appearing to them in an upper room. The gospel is the assertion that this man brought joy to the poor, the damaged and the sinful because he lived and died, and loved and taught, to win them back to the reality of God's unswerving love which nothing we do has the power to alter or destroy.

Jesus said: 'Neither do I condemn you. Go, and do not sin again.' Jesus saw each individual as of unique worth, made in the likeness of God: saw them not as they were but as they might be, as they could be, as one day, by God's grace, each of us will be.

He knew that we cannot be changed by coercion, but only by love. Every parent knows that. And love, that self-giving, forgiving, reconciling love of God that Jesus came to reveal, will in the end prove the most persuasive force in the world if I am to be drawn home to God. That is why God's judgement always goes hand-in-hand with his mercy, and why (where those two conflict) compassion and forgiveness always have the last word. This, above all else, is the powerful gospel that our churches exist to proclaim.

It is only when we know at first hand what it means to forgive and to ask forgiveness of God and of one another and be forgiven, that we shall truly live and convey the heart of the Christian faith. For only in this way are we set free to respond with amazed but increasing thankfulness to the unchanging compassion of the Christlike God.

34

We Shall Be Judged on Love

Lord, that I may receive my sight. Mark 10.51

'I had been blind', she said, 'since early childhood. And then I underwent surgery. When the bandages were removed, I saw this extraordinary sight: four brilliant shafts of light, separated by dark valleys. Puzzled, I turned to a nurse, "What is it?" I asked. "Why," she replied, "you're looking at your fingers".'

That was a woman describing on Radio 4 what it's like suddenly to see the world about us for the first time. Others who were newly sighted described how they had hardly been able to bear the dazzling beauty of trees and flowers and clouds and human faces, and had been quite overwhelmed.

Sadly, for us it is all too familiar. The rapture we feel as children fades, and we are rarely transported by the beauty and wonder on all sides. We take it for granted.

Turn to the New Testament and you will find a significant amount about the recovery of sight: about learning to see. So the blind man Bartimaeus in St Mark's Gospel cries out: 'Lord, help me!' When Jesus insists on stopping and asking what he wants, he replies: 'Lord, that I may receive my sight.'

However, no Gospel incident is as simple as it looks. For what Jesus does is not just to restore physical sight, but to open people's eyes to the reality of God in their midst. Even his closest friends and followers are blind because they lack insight. Only slowly do they begin to notice how Jesus affirms God's love for his creation, every flower and every sparrow, how he pictures God at the heart of such ordinary scenes as the farmer sowing his land or children playing in the marketplace, a shepherd searching for a straying lamb or a father longing for his son to return home. He draws their attention to the mystery, the 'beyond' in their midst, and they watch amazed as he accuses the Pharisees and scribes of having closed minds, or lacking any true insight. And they stand rebuked, his blind disciples, as he says to them: 'You have eyes: can you not see?' In other words: 'Have you no perception, no insight? Can you not see beneath the surface of things and people and glimpse their underlying truth and mystery?'

When much later, with an insight they had failed to achieve while Jesus was with them, the Gospel writers tell his story, one of them describes a very significant healing of another blind man. In fact it is a kind of parable about the degree of perception needed before we can claim to see each other properly: that is to say, seeing each other with the eyes of love, with the eyes of Christ. Jesus takes a blind man by the hand, puts spittle on his eyes, lays his hands on him and asks, 'Can you see anything?' 'I see people,' he replies, 'they look like trees, but they are walking about.' Trees – *things*, objects that may be beautiful but have no feelings. Then Jesus lays his hands on his eyes and only now does he see persons as persons. 'Do you not yet understand?' Jesus asks his followers. 'You have eyes; can you not see?' 'Whereas trees have roots,' writes the critic George Steiner, 'men have legs and are each other's guests.'

'Lord, that I may receive my sight.' What they eventually learned to see when their eyes had been opened, was that Jesus spells out for us in all his words and actions the true nature of God, the true meaning (in Dante's words) of 'the Love that moves the sun and the other stars.' In him Love is defined: St Paul so memorably defines it as 'agape', this self-giving love which is patient and kind, not envious or boastful, conceited or rude; it is never selfish or quick to take offence; it takes no pleasure in the faults of others; it is ready to endure hardship for the sake of truth, giving every person their true worth, seeing each, not as an object by the roadside, which is how the crowd saw Bartimaeus, but seeing him as Jesus saw him, with all his hidden potential as a unique child of God.

'Lord, that I may receive my sight' are words that go to the very heart of our faith. For we need to see ourselves and others not just as we are but as we might be once our inward eyes are cleansed. We are baptized. We are uniquely precious in God's sight. We are forgiven and redeemed. We are made by Love for love, and there is within us a deeply instinctive response to the rightness of St Paul's definition of self-giving love.

Yet even Paul didn't claim that we could ever here achieve the insight and the vision that one day will be ours in heaven. We know our highest truths to be but half-truths, explorations into mystery, that 'now we see through a glass darkly, but only then face to face.' We know, too, that 'Now abideth faith, hope, and love – but the greatest of these is love.'

Why? Because love is the only legal tender in heaven, the only luggage we can take with us when we die. Hope becomes redundant when all we hope for is gained. Faith, that mixture of trust and doubt, will be a thing of the past when we know even as we are known. But love will be the same there as here. All that is truly self-giving love, towards God or towards each other, will survive in heaven, not changed but only increased. For it is the very essence of God himself, and in the words of St John of the Cross, 'When the evening of this life comes, we shall be judged on love.'

35

Commonplace *and* Awesome

And the Word became flesh. John 1.14

If, like me, you date from the year in which Thomas Hardy died and Mickey Mouse was born, then life has changed beyond our wildest imaginings. 'For the worse', we mutter in our Eeyore moods as we recall that vanished world with its very different mores and manners, where there were cinema organs that changed colour, steam trains that ran on time, a less greedy society, a more civilized press. A friend of mine, enthusing to his grandfather about a rough sea, got the response: 'Ah, but you should have seen it in the old days.' But then – despite wars and rumours of wars – you start counting the plusses: the advances in medicine, a free health service, non-invasive surgery, humane treatment of the disabled, hospices, international aid agencies, laws affirming human rights, action to protect the environment, and (not least among the young) a concern for justice for the poor and marginalized. Small signs of God's Kingdom.

If, as you get older you become a littler wiser, something else grows in you: a deeper sense of mystery. You come to understand that to be human is to be full of wonder, faced as we are with the mystery that everything – music, a drop of water or a grain of sand, the migration of a swallow or the birth of a child – everything is at once and the same time both commonplace *and* awesome, and that things are ordinary or extraordinary, simple or complex, according to how much attention you pay to them.

What is more ordinary than stardust? Yet it was stardust falling from the sun untold millennia ago whose atoms and molecules evolved into the intricate marvel that is the natural world, with all its wildness, order and beauty. Stardust which then evolved into the mystery that is me and the mystery that is you: embodied spirits with a haunting sense of God. What is simpler than the uncompromising belief that war is always evil, or more complex than the moral decisions facing a leader who must protect his people from acts of terrorism or the spread of weapons of mass destruction? What are simpler than the words 'I love you', or more mysterious than the transfigured eyes of two people in love? 'What can she see in him, or he in her?' we ask, forgetting that by giving proper attention each sees in the other someone who is unique and wonderful. What is more mundane than home-making, or more profound than the joyful and risky exploration of another's mystery over a lifetime of marriage?

For many of us, it's music and words and art that may have the power to transform the seemingly ordinary into what it truly is: extraordinary. Artists, like mystics, are those who have learned to give attention and, for a moment, lift the veil on that which transcends us. The world says there are limits: but music sings of the ineffable and indefinable, and it is no less real. With simple notes on a parchment Bach creates his *St Matthew Passion*, Mozart his *The Magic Flute*. With the 26 letters of the alphabet Shakespeare explores our human mystery in the guise of *Hamlet* and *King Lear*. With some coloured pigments and a white canvas Rembrandt captures the mystery of old age. Other artists, such as Turner with his use of light or Cezanne with his use of colour, reveal what a poet has called 'the transfigured commonplace': the mystery within every sunrise, every apple, every mountain and every blade of grass. For ours is a sacramental world haunted by God's hidden presence; Gerard Manley Hopkins' 'world charged with the grandeur of God'; one in which, if we have what William Blake called 'cleansed perception', we may find the holy in the ordinary.

Week by week church choirs affirm this in the Sanctus when they sing: 'heaven *and earth* are full of your glory.' Words, sounds, light, matter, people: these are things a child can hear and see, but the wise wonder at – once they have learned to pay attention.

I sometimes think of those who, in an unimaginably different world, watched as the great cathedrals and abbeys grew tall. Theirs, too, was a time of wars and rumours of war: civil war at home, the eve of the Hundred Years' War with France, great famine, and the Black Death which, at a stroke, reduced England's population by a third. They couldn't know that each seemingly solid stone was a spinning mass of electrically charged atoms, nor the size and origin of the universe; nor could they conceive of our post-Darwin, post-Einstein, post-Freudian world of quantum physics and DNA where many mysteries have given up their secrets – and yet not lost their wonder. Other mysteries never will. They remain as hidden to us as they did to all those who have gone before us, and as they will to our children's children: mysteries which have drawn us to a faith where truths are at once simple or beyond our understanding according to how much attention we pay to them. I mean what St Paul calls 'the mystery of our faith.'

For consider: could anything be simpler or more accessible than a baby in a manger, or a man speaking of justice and demonstrating love, or the breaking of bread in a shared meal? What is easier to describe than a cruel and undeserved public death, and an empty grave? Yet look deeper, and words hesitate and stumble and collapse. Indeed, we should have no words to describe God unless (in that deepest mystery of all) 'the Word had been made flesh.' There is no adequate language for the work of the Spirit, the nature of the Eucharist, the meaning of the cross, the appearances of the risen Christ, or the new life of the Kingdom. Yet we preachers, 'stewards of the mysteries', dare to stand in pulpits and struggle to speak of these hidden realities: struggle to convey the reality of a world new-made and potentially transfigured by the grace and goodness of God.

As do the writers of the Gospels. They do so by telling stories of Jesus. Some illustrate his loving and vulnerable humanity. Some are his own stories which point to the secret of the Kingdom, yet others – such as that of his transfiguration – suggest something much more strange. Yes, he was a man, the Word made flesh, but at certain moments they 'beheld his glory', the mystery of his Godlikeness, and it was 'full of grace and truth.' For a moment they saw in Jesus, not (of course) the unimaginable glory of what it means to be God, but traces of that glory, and something too of the glory of the human, created in God's likeness, and it was a blinding revelation. In him they saw their true potential and so – by implication – the world transfigured. It's a poor analogy, perhaps, but I liken it to going in the early morning to the Lady Chapel of Salisbury Cathedral in winter, when the east window is a jigsaw of indecipherable dark shapes, but then, as the sun comes up, it is slowly transfigured in all its scarlets and greens and blues. It is still a puzzling jigsaw from outside, but from the inside it shows the mystery of suffering men and women enveloped in the light of that central figure on the cross.

On Ash Wednesday many of us have our forehead marked with ash and hear the words, 'Remember that you are dust and to dust you shall return.' But remember you are dust with a difference: dust for whom the whole creation was made. Troubled dust that dreams and falls in love and creates music and art and responds to beauty. Dust that worships and has occasional glimpses of glory. Dust, in the words of the Prayer Book collect, that is to be 'changed into Christ's likeness, from glory to glory.' Dust that travels between doubt and faith, between weakness and transfiguration.

To be a follower of Christ is not about rewards and punishments, nor is it about saying the creed with your fingers crossed at certain uncomfortable bits. It is about trusting that at the heart of the mystery there is the self-giving love of God. It is about desiring to respond to that love, and so slowly, infinitely slowly – so slowly that we may not notice – being changed, transfigured if you like, into our true human likeness, *his* likeness. Perhaps as the season of Epiphany gives way to Lent we should think on these things, and seek to develop two unfashionable qualities which bring us closer to God: a sense of wonder, and a grateful heart.

Scripture Index